INSPIRATIONAL YOUTH

>>> →

TRANSFORMING AVERAGE *to* EXTRAORDINARY

Authors:

DR. MARINA V. GILLMORE

DR. MONIQUE R. HENDERSON

KEITH L. BROWN

Telling the inspirational stories of:

MaryPat Hector - Joe Gigunito - Max Wallack
Jordan Howard - Shaylee Hatch - R.L. Wilson

With a foreword by:
Dr. Robert Denham,
Retired Dean of the University of Redlands School of Education

Published by The Institute for Educational and Social Justice

Printed by Booklogix Publishing Services

ISBN# 978-0-9890453-0-8

Printed in the United States of America

Library of Congress Control Number: 2013933681

The Institute for Educational and Social Justice Press
700 E. Redlands Blvd, Suite U #293
Redlands, CA 92373

INSPIRATIONAL
YOUTH

>>> ———————————→

TRANSFORMING AVERAGE
to **EXTRAORDINARY**

TABLE OF CONTENTS

DEDICATION

For Joe, Jordan, MaryPat, Max, R.L., and Shaylee.

May your voices, vision, and purpose be only strengthened as you continue to grow up in this world, with all its beauty, hope, and confusion. The poet Max Ehrmann may have said it best in his poem Desiderata that "with all its shams, drudgery, and broken dreams, it is still a beautiful world."

Thank you for reminding us on a daily basis just what this beauty can look like. Thank you for sharing your stories with us so honestly and forthrightly.

This book belongs to you and your futures.

AUTHORS' NOTE

When we started work on this book, we knew there would be a sense of urgency to write and publish it in a timely manner. We knew young people change so rapidly, and we wanted the stories of the young people featured here to be relevant, not only to their own lives, but to the larger context in which they were living, learning, and leading. But life sometimes throws us curve balls, and this book ended up taking a lot longer to write and publish than we had originally intended. We thought about going back in and updating all of the stories presented here, because we knew that a seventeen-year-old college freshman might look back at what he said when he was fifteen years old and cringe just a little bit, noting that in two years his perspective had changed significantly.

We decided, however, to tell the stories as they were told to us, in one moment in time. This decision was an intentional one that we feel warrants a word of further explanation. We know we could have spent more time bringing the stories up to date. As you'll note from the brief updates we provided at the end of every chapter, we would have had more than enough material to work with. But we chose the alternate route because we believe in the power of MaryPat at thirteen years old, and Joe at fifteen, and Jordan at nineteen. We also believe in them at fifteen, seventeen, and twenty-one, respectively. And we will continue to believe in them as they mature into increasingly complex individuals with the passing of years. We hope this world is as kind and generous to them as they have been to this world so far.

We also realize we could have painted more complete pictures of these young people's lives by extending the focus of their stories beyond the immediate contexts of their own voices. We are well aware that we could have done more extensive research – sought interviews and testimonials from the adults who know them well. However, we chose not to because we wanted these stories to be largely theirs and theirs alone. We wanted authenticity and relevance. We believe strongly that too often the voices of young people are drowned out in our adult-centric society. Whether this is a result of our own insecurities as adults, or our collective consciousness that tells us that youth need to "know their place" and "wait their turn," we want to challenge those insecurities, and that collective consciousness, with this book. For that reason, among others, we left the interviews with adults for another book, another day, another time – because this is the young people's time. This is the time of these young leaders who – like countless other youth – are told by adults to wait until they get "into the real world." After reading their stories on the pages that follow, we hope you discover that their "real world" is the same world we live in now. And it is in this real world that they are working to shape a better future for us all.

Our greatest hope is that we have done these incredible young people justice, that we have told their stories in ways that are both honest and true-to-form, and that their voices, hopes, and dreams for a better future for this world shine through loud and clear. Any omissions, mistakes, or misrepresentations are ours and ours alone.

FOREWORD

Young people so often get attention for negative things. Almost all of us have heard troubling stories about the plight of our youth, shared repeatedly through the traditional media, social networking, and word of mouth. And most of us have been personally touched somehow by the irresponsible or, more tragically, dangerous decisions of a young person – whether it be a young man who walks into a school and commits mass murder or a niece who gets in trouble at school for cyber-bullying.

These stories and experiences haunt us. They make us fearful, and – as they should – they strike us at the very core of our beings.

But as a former Southern California high school principal who has worked at both comprehensive and alternative public high schools and a retired college professor and university dean, I can tell you that these are not the only stories out there. There are other stories that need to be told.

While I hear the stories of tragedy, and have known many of these troubled youth firsthand, I also know of countless young people who have dedicated themselves to improving the world around them and advancing causes of social and educational justice.

I have had the opportunity to learn about young people who have helped to build houses for low-income, working-class families.

I have seen teens tirelessly tutor children who are struggling academically, socially, and emotionally. I've learned about youth-run programs to bring water to impoverished third world communities.

In my moments of despair and discouragement, it is these young people who have encouraged and challenged me the most.

More of us need to hear these stories. We need to be reassured that all is not wrong in the world – and that the future is far brighter than some would have us believe.

As adults, we need to hear these stories so that we are not guilty of setting low expectations for the young people around us. While teens and young adults certainly need to be shown grace and understanding as they grow, we also should expect them to be kind and empathetic, to have hearts of service, and to be interested in giving back to a world that, so often, has given a lot to them already. When we hold these positive expectations for our youth, young people will respond beyond what we even dare to imagine.

The young people around us desperately need to hear these stories, too. Research tells us about the realities of "social norming" – the idea that individuals respond to their perceptions about what other people similar to them are doing.

If our young people believe that most teens are living lives devoid of virtue and meaning, they will be far more likely to choose such lives themselves. But if they understand that they have peers who are working hard, using their creativity and innovation to help others and make the world a dramatically better place, then they are likely to make similar choices in their own lives.

The sharing of these stories and ideas is exactly how social justice movements among youth are started – and how they are spread.

The authors of this book are people I respect tremendously. They recognize the importance of telling the stories of people who are not always heard and acknowledged in our society and have made this an essential part of their life's work. And they tell stories honestly and powerfully. Their work compels me to make a difference in my society and world. I know, through this work, they will challenge you to do more, too.

The six young people highlighted in this book have truly transformational stories. They remind us of the tremendous power and promise of youth. They challenge all of us – whatever our age and background – to make the most of the time, talents and other resources we have been given. And they inspire us to advance important social and educational justice causes in our own communities, our nation, and beyond.

I hope that you enjoy getting to know the young people highlighted in this book. I know that I have.

Dr. Robert Denham, Retired Dean of the
University of Redlands School of Education

INTRODUCTION:
A CALL *to* THE READER

The premise of this book is simple – take six amazing young people who have inspired us both personally and professionally, and tell their stories. The implications, however, are much more complex.

When we first started hearing about the remarkable work that some of the young people profiled in this book were doing, we were eager to tell others.

And as we worked with school and non-profit organization leaders nationwide, that is exactly what we did. We started sharing anecdotal experiences and video clips featuring the young people about whom we were writing.

Yet, when we began to tell our stories of young people who are changing their communities – and the greater world – in big ways, we were met with some interesting reactions. On one hand, teachers, counselors, parents, administrators, non-profit leaders, and others responsible for working with youth were very excited to learn about these young people and their work. But at the same time, we also encountered a surprising amount of skepticism from others in the same fields, whose concerns sounded something like this:

"You know a kid who runs orphanages in Africa? Wow. That's great. But you know what? I don't think the students we work with here are really like that. They are just average kids – not the kinds of kids who go out and try to do things to change the world."

Or like this:

"That's great, but you don't understand the population of students we work with *here*. These are poor kids. Some of our students can't even read. They are thinking about feeding *themselves,* not children in Africa."

These responses, heard repeatedly in some variation or another, led us to think about and question the notion of the "average kid." Who is really the average kid? What does that label even mean? And why are the expectations for most young people so low? The reactions we encountered also led us to think deeply about the labels we place on children from admittedly disadvantaged backgrounds, and the ways in which these labels often stay with young people as they transition into adulthood.

At the same time as we were meeting with negativity from some of the adult leaders we serve, we were also seeing similar messages portrayed in the media.

Judging by the stories in the news, the current generation of young people is a frustrating and hopeless lot – a group whose brains are addled by drugs, alcohol, bath salts, household cleaning products, and any other substances available for abuse. When they are not dropping out of school or failing state mandated tests, the media would have us believe that today's youth are busy using recent advances in technology to engage in sexting or cyber-bullying. The media maintain that today's young people are to be feared for their defiance, their lack of empathy, and a disinterest in work or personal advancement.

What should we do, we wondered, with this disconnect?

We decided, after much reflection, reading, and intellectual and moral grappling that we wanted to challenge the notion of the "average kid" entirely.

We refuse to believe that some youth, by nature of their intellect, upbringing, zip code, or values, are somehow exceptional and capable of transforming the world, while other young people – the majority of them – are just mediocre and not capable of much. We soundly reject this notion, and all its inherent biases, because we believe it to be ethically wrong. And, just as importantly, we reject this notion because we have seen differently and we know differently.

When we have gone into schools from Southern California to Atlanta to Houston and everywhere in between, we have not met any "average kids" – the sort of young people who keep expectations low. Instead, the young people we have met at every stop along the way have been overflowing with the potential –

and desire – to create tremendous change in their schools, their communities, and far beyond. And many young people are successfully affecting change. Some, like the ones profiled in this book, do it through organized systems that they have established and helped to put into place. Others bring about change in ways that are not as systemic. But they are still working quietly behind the scenes, encouraging their peers to make good choices, serving as positive examples for others, and steadfastly focusing on goals they have set for themselves.

At the same time, we hope to move beyond simply bridging the divide between who today's young people are and how they are viewed by the adults around them, as well as society at large. Ultimately, we also hope this book can become a powerful tool to encourage both young people and the adults in their lives to take the risks involved in seeing their visions of positive change come to fruition.

By highlighting the work of the six young people profiled in this book, we hope that we can engage in small-scale positive social norming – making the work those profiled are doing seem more like the standard for youth, instead of simply an inspirational exception meant only for an elite few. As young people and the adults who care about them are able to see the good work that is being done, they also may be encouraged to dedicate themselves to their own projects, working to strengthen their schools, their communities, their places of worship, and beyond. When educational and social justice work is seen as doable – and is supported in the broader society – more young people are likely to have the courage to act on their values and ideas in powerful, transformational ways.

The young people we got to know during the writing of this book have some compelling and challenging messages to share about their generation.

In many ways, it seems as if today's young people have a great deal in common with the generations that have come before them. They hold a strong sense of idealism and a certainty that they can and should have a hand in changing the world for the better. They believe that they have the power to bring about change, and that they have a moral obligation to do their part to leave the world a better place for the generations that follow. They also respect the adults who are in their lives and are quick to seek their guidance and expertise. Even when young people seem to have found many of the answers themselves, they are eager to have their ideas affirmed by adults. And they want to know that they are supported, whether they succeed or fail.

At the same time, this generation is a particularly unique one.

Technology has made this an especially exciting and liberating time to be young. Today's youth do not need lessons on how to use technology – they, for the most part, intuitively know how to use such tools to their benefit because they grew up using them. As digital natives, information is easy for them to access. There is no need to ask for a ride to the nearest city library. They do not have to wait for an opportunity to ask a particularly informed teacher for specific information. All of this is available to most of today's young people with just a few clicks or keystrokes.

Interestingly, as we were gathering data for this book, we often found that the young people who we interviewed had collected about as much information on us as we had about them. They were familiar with our research interests, our academic and personal backgrounds, and the focus of *The Institute for Educational and Social Justice*. And collecting this information was not something they were directed by adults to do. Conversely, the research was something that came quite naturally to them and was done quickly and easily, as they also worked on homework, texted friends, or downloaded their favorite new songs.

Today's technology does not merely give young people access to information – it gives them access to connections. Youth today are not limited to finding like-minded individuals in their high schools. Instead, they can use social networking tools to link up with peers – and renowned experts in their field of interest – from the next neighborhood over, or from halfway around the world. Young people were once limited in their interactions with those of like minds, being forced to wait for some specialized camp, class, or after-school program to meet. But now, they can connect and communicate around the clock, and often do.

The young people profiled in this book also share another interesting similarity – the lack of fear of making mistakes. Possibly because they have become comfortable putting their thoughts and ideas in front of a broad online audience, they are not particularly afraid to look like "failures" for taking on a project that does not work. Instead, they seem to take action quickly, rallying people to their causes and figuring out much of what they are doing by feel, as they go along. Because they do not fear being wrong, they also seem to have a heightened sense of humility, making them more willing to make and learn from their mistakes and from others.

We are excited for you to "meet" these young people, to hear and understand their stories, largely told in their own voices. We are also excited to consider how you – as parents, youth leaders, or young people yourselves – might learn from them and be inspired by what they have to share.

As we indicated, the young people profiled in this book are really just "average kids" in many ways. There are easily thousands of others doing similar projects, although not always with the same degree of success as the six highlighted here. But we chose these six to be representative of the broader population – of young people everywhere who are, day by day, making the world a better place through their hard work, their advocacy, and their ingenuity.

The young people profiled in this book are as follows: Joe Gigunito of Montoursville, Pennsylvania (*Where Is the Love Foundation*); Jordan Howard of Los Angeles, California (*Jordan Inspires*); MaryPat Hector of Atlanta, Georgia (*Youth In Action* Founder and National President of the *National Action Network's YouthMove*); Max Wallack of Natick, Massachusetts (*Puzzles to Remember*); R.L. Wilson of Indio, California (*Brothers Amazingly and Intellectually Talented*); and Shaylee Hatch of Nampa, Idaho (*The Temporary Home Foundation*). Some are running full-blown non-profits with national recognition, while others are just beginning to shape their passion and talents into organizations that will likely gain formal non-profit status in the near future.

We selected each of them for inclusion in this book because we saw something refreshingly genuine in their stories. We also saw an alignment between what they said they did and what they actually did. In other words, our background research confirmed that these young people were acting on their beliefs in powerful ways – they weren't just sitting around talking about change, they were making it happen.

And maybe, at a more basic level, their stories have compelled us to live better lives. As we face tough decisions in our own work, we often find ourselves saying, "What would Joe do in this situation?" or "I know that MaryPat would have no fear in tackling this issue head on."

In the coming chapters, we will give you a better understanding of the background of each of these young people, the work that they are doing, what inspires them during difficult times, and what they hope to achieve in the future.

We also will explore the role that technology plays in the lives of young people, and how each of these young leaders regards society's views of their generation. Additionally, we will share information elicited from each of these individuals, outlining ways that adults and young people can connect with, encourage, and motivate other youth in their lives.

Our hope is that you find the same inspiration in these young people's stories as we do. But we also hope you do not place them up on an unreachable pedestal. They wouldn't want to be viewed that way. Joe, Jordan, MaryPat, Max, R.L., and Shaylee want to be part of the conversation. They want you to see a little bit of yourself and others in each of their stories.

We must also acknowledge, however, that in the stories that follow we chose to capture a unique, and fleeting, moment in the lives of each of these young leaders. Since we initially spent time with them, getting to know them and their stories, they have changed, and evolved, and – yes – grown up even more. These stories, then, are not meant to be comprehensive biographies of the young people, but rather special glimpses into their hearts and minds during the times in their lives that they were gracious and trusting enough to share their stories with us and the world.

Because of their trust and generosity, we are indebted to the young people featured here, who we now view as not only inspiring leaders of their own generation, but also as colleagues of ours. See, our stories may all be different, but our vision is the same – to create opportunities and avenues of hope for others. We believe that when we are able to come together in powerful and meaningful ways, often through the currency of stories, we are redefining what it means to be human and what it means to bring about real and lasting change.

CHAPTER ONE

JOE GIGUNITO
MONTOURSVILLE, PENNSYLVANIA
Where is the Love Foundation

Early Fall 2011, Age 15

"I got kind of teary-eyed because I looked out at these kids and saw how much potential they had. But I also saw how many of them were not living up to their potential."

The first time we met Joe, we were wrapping up a weeklong program evaluation in Williamsport, Pennsylvania.

We walked into a school cafeteria to see a young man wearing jeans and a black t-shirt with a picture of the African continent on it, speaking to an audience of about thirty upper elementary and junior high students.

Joe never raised his voice or resorted to dramatic gimmicks to hold the attention of his young audience. And yet, they all appeared mesmerized by what he had to say. We soon learned that Joe is the founder of the *Where is the Love Foundation*, which funds orphanages in Kenya. The five orphanages serve 112 students, who receive daily care, support, and schooling. The orphanages employ fifteen people, including teachers, housekeepers, and guardians. The students who attend the orphanages include many who became orphans after their parents died or became unable to support them due to terminal illnesses or other tragedies.

When Joe talked about his inspiration for starting the organization, his speech quickened and the excitement in his voice was almost palpable:

"This journey has been so cool," he said, adding that his inspiration came when he was a seventh-grader attending a convention called the *NextGen Summit* in Anaheim, California. Interestingly, the tone for his work was actually set by the U2 song *Beautiful Day*, which was played to establish the atmosphere for conference events. "I think hearing that first song from U2 really set the tone for how I've been able to direct my passions through *Where is the Love*. I was sitting at the *NextGen Summit* and this young man came out to the stage. At fifteen years old he was standing there and talking about abolishing slavery in Darfur. And I was just so inspired by this young person who was willing and able to stand in front of thousands of people – 30,000 teenagers from all over the country – just telling his story and how he's been able to change the world one step at a time. That was so inspiring to me!"

His experience at the conference stuck with him, and when Joe got home, he found himself researching U2 and the work that lead singer Bono was doing in Africa.

"I thought, 'Wow!' This was really different for me to see a rock band so involved with non-profit work, because you usually sit back and look at a rock band and your first thought is drugs, sex and money. So it was interesting to see how in all the research I was doing on this band, I wasn't finding much of the typical drug, sex and money stuff. The main thing I was getting from my U2 research was just positive energy. Bono has just really inspired me to be myself and not care what other people think about me and to do what my heart tells me to do."

Joe shared that his heart told him he needed to do more to improve the world and that his focus should be on the orphans in Kenya.

"When I am working with *Where is the Love*, when I am really focused and moving forward," he said, "it makes me feel that in my heart I've done something right for the world. And at the end of the day, knowing that you've done something right for the world just might be the greatest accomplishment of all."

Joe founded the *Where is the Love* Foundation with a very succinct, yet profound, mission – to end extreme poverty in Africa. The first *Where is the Love* orphanage opened in the Kathonzweni District near Nairobi, Kenya, due in large part to the relationship Joe was able to establish with Liz Mueni. A native of Nairobi, Liz was already running an orphanage in Kenya when Joe met her and heard her express her funding needs to keep the orphanage open. *Where is the Love* soon took on the charge of providing all the funding needed for Liz to continue the good work she was already doing. From there, the partnership between Liz and *Where is the Love* continued to grow and flourish.

Running an organization while in high school is no easy feat. On a typical day, Joe checks in both before and after school on *Where is the Love* business, firing off texts, social network messages, and emails. Often, these communications are focused on fundraising efforts, while at other times he hears from potential donors interested in learning more about the organization, its mission and how it operates. Sometimes, he handles logistical questions about fundraising events or schedules interviews and speaking engagements for himself and other volunteer members of his team.

There are days when his schoolwork feels like a hindrance to his fundraising efforts – even though he fully recognizes that an education is the key to his long-term success and credibility.

"Definitely the hardest challenge for me is balancing everything in my life because there's so much that has to be done and there's not enough time to do it, so all my homework, all the WITL (*Where is the Love*) stuff, all this, all that – I have to find a way to balance it all out or nothing will get done," he said. "So I really think balance has become a key challenge in my life – figuring out how to maintain everything at a stable level."

Seeing the Positives in Trying Times

Joe is an intensely reflective young man – something that became clear almost immediately upon meeting him.

He thinks and talks often about three events that have shaped his life in irreversible ways – the death of his fifteen-year-old brother, Nate, when he was eight years old, his father's twenty-plus year addiction to heroin, and his parents' divorce.

"Everything in my life I know has happened for a specific reason," he said confidently.

His brother, Nate, died in 2004 of AML leukemia. The timeframe leading up to Nate's death was a heart-wrenching one for Joe and the rest of his family.

"My brother's illness played a huge role in my maturity," he said. "I would stay home for days at a time taking care of myself, making lunch, doing my homework. I grew up so much quicker than I really should have. It was hard, but it happened for a reason. I have to believe and know that."

He shared that his father, a former heroin addict who was once homeless and is now an active leader in the Williamsport recovery community, is one of his biggest heroes.

"My biggest inspiration is my dad," he said. "I look at him, living on the streets and then changing his life, helping people, becoming a very successful businessman, and it really makes me think about success and the fact that I want to be successful – to do something on my own that I can be proud to have achieved."

Interestingly, he also said that his parents' divorce has aided him in some ways, by allowing him to benefit from the strengths of each of his parents' specific parenting and personality styles.

"I like staying with my mom during the week because she's always on me – 'Hey, are you doing this, are you doing that?' and she reinforces what I do with school and with *Where is the Love*, and supports me in so many other ways, too. I know she wants what's best for me and I really appreciate her staying on top of me because if I get off track she's right there to put me back on track."

Yet, he said that staying with his father on the weekends also is a very good thing, because his father's more relaxed parenting style gives him the freedom he needs to learn and grow in other ways.

"He's just a good, laid back guy," he said.

Success as a Team

Joe said that his vision for his organization is to serve the needs of orphans in Kenya in a way that is strategic and also team-oriented.

He shared that his organization's success is about "coming together, starting a project, and then completing that project." He said often, adding new people to a group – or achieving even small accomplishments together – can quickly snowball, creating more and more success.

"The changes and accomplishments of a group can ultimately result in excitement and being able to move forward with the group's goals and stir everyone up to do more than they even thought possible in the beginning," he said. He added that, as a leader, he strives to allow people to use their own strengths and to seek out people who have the talents and knowledge that his organization requires.

The non-profit founder said he has been challenged to rethink how he defines success in the past few years, particularly as he has watched his father achieve financial success.

"I had to see for myself that money really isn't what people think it is," he acknowledged. "It's not the most important thing. I don't like going on shopping sprees or anything. That's not me, personally. I really look at that and say I do want to make my own money so that I can be self-reliant. I am driven because I want to do that – I want to make my own. And I really think my dad plays a huge role in why I'm so motivated to do the things that I do."

Learning from Mistakes

Joe was quick to admit he has made mistakes in his organization – particularly early in its history.

He said one of *Where is the Love*'s biggest errors early on was not teaching and equipping his volunteers to use a detailed, universal system for selling *Where is the Love* merchandise, which serves as one of the organization's primary sources of funding. He also believes that he should have done a better job of monitoring volunteers to prevent stealing or misplacing of monies raised.

"I'd have guys go out and sell things, but then never write down the orders," he recalled. "We would never fulfill that person's order and it started to get disorienting. People would call me and want to know where their sweatshirt was and I didn't even know. I had to let some kids go because they were trying to steal and it was really starting to get bad. I caught it and we got a better system of things going and today it's better. But it is one of my biggest regrets."

Because he has chosen to take on such a visible role, speaking in front of crowds of as many as 5,000 people at a time, Joe also has opened himself up to criticism – both from his peers and from total strangers.

But he said he believes the criticism helps far more than it hurts.

"Criticism really shapes me," he maintained. "I think criticism motivates me so much more to do what I want to do because criticism, to me, is usually just the other person's jealousy of how successful you've become. I actually like when people criticize me because I take it and run with it and it really motivates me to want to do more."

Interestingly, one of his earliest critics is now his booking agent.

"She came up to me and said 'You will never make it,'" he recalled. "I thought, 'Wow, my so-called friend would tell me to my face I wouldn't make it?' Today that girl is in charge of all my bookings and speaking engagements. And I've told her that it's not fair that she told me that, but look what I did? I took that criticism and I ran with it and look where I am today. It's one situation that really motivated me to do more. I'll never forget it. I'll never forget it."

Joe is quick to recognize both his strengths and his weaknesses – and he has no problem delegating work in areas he does not feel are his strengths. When we met him, in fact, he immediately explained that he respects writers – and that he has someone on his volunteer staff to handle his writing.

But speaking to people, in groups both large and small, is a clear strength and one that helps him to communicate the vision and needs of his organization effectively.

"To me, any size crowd feels like five people in the room," he said. "I void out all the eyes staring at me and I think about that life-changing day when I was in seventh grade at the convention and that young man came out and spoke in front of 30,000 people. I think about that and I mold myself out of that. I think speaking is my biggest strength."

Interestingly, when he looks at his achievements, one he prizes most highly was the opportunity to return to his middle school and speak.

"I remember being in seventh grade and being told I couldn't do anything and that really motivated me," he said. "Then, I got invited back a couple years later to speak. When I first started speaking that day, I got kind of teary-eyed because I looked out at these kids and saw how much potential they had. But I also saw how many of them were not living up to their potential. And I loved the way it felt to be back in my middle school speaking to those kids."

On his Generation

While Joe said he sees a great deal of potential, he also sees a certain apathy plaguing his generation – particularly among students from high-income families.

"I see a lot of my peers who rely on their dads who are lawyers or doctors or millionaires and can afford to give them everything and anything they want. I don't really like that. My dad has worked hard and we're a successful family, but I don't want to rely on my dad for the rest of my life. I really think that today many teenagers aren't into social justice work because mentally you have to be on top of what you're doing and what you're talking about. When I recruit people to *Where is the Love*, they're kind of hesitant at first because they know the work they're going to have to put in in order to get on the same page as me and the other members of *Where is the Love*."

He said sometimes he worries that technology may hinder his generation's face-to-face communication skills.

"The kids are at home, inside on their computers. They text; they don't call each other anymore. And you can see that over time, it's pretty much a characteristic of evolution because we've changed from calling to texting to Facebook. And you can see how people have really gotten away from talking on the phone or in person."

Still, Joe posited that technology is a powerful tool and that technological proficiency is essential.

"I don't think you can be successful without having it in today's world," he said. "Social media has taken over so much in our lives that it's unreal. I research a lot of things – it's what I love doing. I'm really into Facebook. I know a lot about it and to me it's important because it's the way we communicate. Teenagers respond quicker to social networking than they do in person because there's not that awkward meeting. But on the computer, they're by themselves. They get to interact with *Where is the Love* on their terms."

What Adults Need to Know

Joe said that he respects his parents' generation, but also thinks that sometimes they should clear the way and give young people more freedom to fail.

"I think that today's parents really need to let teenagers try things for themselves," he said. "Let the child fall and get themselves back up. Because telling them not to do something will make them upset and make them want to do it even more. I've experienced that and it's frustrating. I want to go out and try new things. If I fall, I'll get back up. It's as easy as that."

He said risk-taking can be a strength, provided young people are not engaging in self-destructive behaviors.

"A lot of parents really don't want their kids to take that risk," he acknowledged. "But I'm really against that. I think that parents and teachers should let kids try things out and see what can happen. You never know if you'll be the next Justin Bieber. You never know if you'll be the next Bono. You don't know, but taking a risk could ultimately change that, so I think that's really important."

He said his generation is excited by rewards and achievement.

"Rewards really spark people's attention and make them want to do more," he added.

He said he wishes he could get more adults to put themselves in the place of teenagers when working with them in leadership roles.

"An adult has to go back to a teenage mindset for a connection to happen," he said. "You have to be able to think back to when you were a teenager and how you acted. It's the only way parents and teachers can maintain stable relationships with teenagers."

Looking Ahead

Joe definitely is not a young person who believes he has every step of his future mapped out. He is interested in being a professional musician and a Harvard-educated doctor, among other things. But he also said he is confident in his desire to continue to advance *Where is the Love* well into his adulthood.

"Going to Harvard, earning a doctorate degree, what could I do for Africa then? I could take *Where is the Love* to a whole new level – not just with the orphanages, but also with AIDS clinics. That's what really motivates me on a day-to-day basis. Sometimes the days are hard, but I keep pushing and trying because I have that idea – that goal and focus."

Joe was not always sold on the importance of a Harvard education, or on any college education at all.

But then, he said that he recognized the credibility he could potentially bring to his work with *Where is the Love* and beyond.

"Going to Harvard would then set the standard as to who we are as *Where is the Love*," he remarked. "You know, it would show that

I'm serious about what I'm doing and that I care about my grades and that I care about being successful. But ultimately, to me it shows everyone what I can do in the world with that education. I'm really excited about taking this challenge on and pursuing it. It's not going to be easy – I intend it not to be – but in the end it's going to be so rewarding."

Update

We interviewed Joe for this book in the summer of 2011. Since that time, quite a few things have changed in his life. Joe is now an eleventh grader and is thinking more seriously about his post-high school plans. Joe recently shared with us that *Where is the Love* currently has five orphanages operating in Africa, and Joe hopes to continue to expand his work. His junior year of high school has been a tough one, particularly since his father was diagnosed with congestive heart failure. Between classwork, his work sustaining the orphanages, and helping to encourage and support his father, he has taken great solace in the support of his friends and family. He has also been exploring both local and national music scenes, and currently serves a manager for a group of hip-hop musicians. Joe says he is not sure what the future holds for him, but he knows he wants *Where is the Love* to continue to expand and serve as many children as possible.

CHAPTER TWO

JORDAN HOWARD
LOS ANGELES, CALIFORNIA
Jordan Inspires

Early Fall 2011, Age 19

"When you have low expectations for someone, of course they're going to play out, they're not going to perform. When you have high expectations – that's one of the things that I learned in school – when you have high expectations for us we'll rise to those expectations."

We first met Jordan when she was nineteen years old and a sophomore at Santa Monica College.

We had heard a great deal about her environmental justice and environmental activism work from community leaders and social networking activity, and were eager to learn more about her efforts, her convictions, and what motivated her to continue.

We were thankful to find that she was just as eager as we were to get the conversation started.

From the first time we met, we knew that she would have a part in this book. Her determination to educate and serve others was immediately clear. She was enigmatic in a way – somehow both unassuming and commanding in her presence at the same time.

Challenging Questions, Transformational Answers

For high school, Jordan found herself attending an environmental charter high school in Lawndale, California, a community located in South Los Angeles.

Jordan and her family did not seek out the charter school because of its environmental emphasis. Instead, they felt that the school was one of Jordan's few opportunities to attend a public high school that would adequately prepare her for college. That was because the sprawling neighborhood high school she was zoned to attend was a dropout factory, where just over fifty percent of students graduated from high school and a large percentage of teens did not stay in school long enough to see the start of their junior year.

"My neighborhood school didn't graduate many of its students," Jordan explained. "It was not a good school at all. So, this charter school was small. It was a really close-knit community school and it was focused on getting kids to college. My parents liked that, so there I went."

Interestingly, Jordan was initially reluctant to embrace the environmental focus of her new high school, viewing it as something that she basically had to tolerate in order to receive a quality education and escape her troubled neighborhood school.

Her freshman year, Jordan took an environmental science class that chronicled the causes and effects of global warming.

Jordan was one of the students who frequently asked her teacher – and fellow students with environmental orientations – tough questions about environmentalism.

"I used to always be the one, the only one actually, who would raise my hand and question the teacher's lesson on global warming, telling her, 'You know, we shouldn't be forced to learn about environmental activism and you're just indoctrinating us to be hippies.'" Jordan shared that when her class would go on field trips to the Ballona Wetlands, she was always questioning the employees there: "I'd question them, 'Why is this important? Shouldn't there be other things that the city should fund?' And I really was resistant to the green movement, of course, until my tenth grade year."

She said her frustration stemmed from the feeling that so much of what she was hearing was negative and restrictive, focusing on a long list of "should nots" that felt unrealistic and out of touch with the goals of the typical person in an industrialized society.

Then, in tenth grade, Jordan was required to take an environmental service learning class called Green Ambassadors. She expected the class to be another exercise in frustration – one where she completed more of her graduation requirements without learning much that she would carry with her into adulthood, or even into her home life while in high school.

But Jordan was pleasantly surprised by her experience in the Green Ambassadors program, quickly finding herself moving beyond the litany of grim, gloom-and-doom environmental messages she had been hearing and resisting for so long.

Jordan said that, "We learned about global warming, but we also learned about solutions. We learned about solar energy, electric cars, and organic food. We learned about more than the problems, we learned about solutions and then we were empowered to teach the solutions not only in our school, but in our community."

She shared that this was the first time she remembers really being able to think beyond environmental problems to viable solutions: "Before this class, I remember feeling like people were just pointing fingers at me and saying, 'You're a horrible person because you drive everywhere. You're a horrible person because you don't eat organic food, or granola, or drive a VW.'"

But in the Green Ambassadors class, Jordan said she became inspired to bring about change in real, meaningful, and tangible ways.

"I was inspired because I saw that it wasn't that I didn't care before. I was resistant to the green movement because I didn't know. It was simply that I didn't know how bad my lifestyle was for the planet and for myself. And so when I learned about viable solutions, I was really empowered to share them. I was empowered to share them with my family and friends. I began to take on the challenge of educating people about environmental problems and solutions, but really focusing on the solutions to empower them to live sustainable lifestyles. I saw that sustainability wasn't only good for the environment, it was good for my health and it was good for my pocketbook. I learned that it could be cheaper to grow my own food at home and that it was cheaper to go to thrift stores and buy clothes."

She grew quiet for a moment, before sharing a simple, but profound reflection: "I don't know, I was really inspired by that."

Finding Motivation and Carrying it Forward

Jordan said that her work is motivated by the connection she shares with her three-year-old sister, who is sixteen years her junior.

"My sister came three years ago by surprise. It was a surprise to everyone. I mean, I'm nineteen and I have a three-year-old sister, so it was definitely a surprise to my parents. And I think being around my sister and teaching her and seeing everything she learns from my parents and me just shows me how much of an impact education can have. How much of an impact being around someone and their actions can have. She says everything I say, whether it's good or bad, so she just motivates me to be a better person. She motivates me to teach her more and to make sure that my actions are all positive around her."

After what Jordan described as her "environmental epiphany" when she was fifteen, she became increasingly focused on meeting a need she saw in terms of the lack of environmental education within the green movement.

"That's when I vowed to focus on educating people about the solutions to environmental issues – educating people through film, speeches, workshops, and through my own sustainable lifestyle."

Jordan directed some of her efforts into filmmaking. "I began directing short films," she said, "and using the power of filmmaking to engage youth and adults on environmental issues affecting their communities. The green movement has failed to connect its movement to the social justice movement, when there are direct causations. Growing up in South Los Angeles, illnesses like asthma, diabetes, and high cholesterol seem natural. I seriously thought these illnesses were genetic. When I began to learn about my relation to the environment and environmental justice, however, it took my activism to another level. Learning about how economically disadvantaged people are at a greater risk of environmental degradation because of their economic status made my skin boil!"

Jordan took her anger and channeled it into further educating others.

"It became another opportunity to educate. I knew if I could educate community members on toxic waste, we could mobilize against toxic corporations that target and pollute poor communities. Like Van Jones says, 'You can't trash the planet without trashing people. And you can't trash people without trashing the planet.'"

Jordan uses her oratory skills to motivate and inspire youth to action. "Using my public speaking skills," she explained, "I've facilitated international youth summits with *5 Gyres* and the *Algalita Marine Research Foundation*. In March 2011, we flew in 120 students, ranging in age from ten to eighteen and representing fourteen countries and five continents. Over the course of a weekend, students learned facts about and solutions to global plastic pollution and worked with their peers to brainstorm the best projects to implement in their own communities. It was important that we did not give the students the answers to cleaning up their communities, as Nairobi has different problems than Indonesia or Chicago. Every solution has to be perfect for the community in which it's being implemented."

Through her younger sister, Jordan said she has been honored to witness the influence that education – particularly education delivered in a loving, compassionate way – can have on individuals and also, in turn, on groups of people.

Jordan also recognizes the impact that teachers and education have had on her own life.

She said the adults who reached her most effectively were those who took the time to get to know her, while also revealing key elements of themselves, who they were, and what motivated them.

She noted that she was inspired by "teachers who weren't just teachers. In elementary school, my third grade teacher – I'll never forget it – she used to tell us that she wasn't our friend, she was our teacher."

Jordan said she found the teacher's detachment a bit off-putting, even while recognizing that the teacher was trying to make the point that her top goal was to educate them.

At her charter high school, she commented that her teachers had a very different attitude toward their students and the work that they were doing.

"In high school most of my teachers were mentors. So they weren't just teachers for an hour or so and then it was like, 'Okay, after social studies I'm done.' They were mentors to us, and seeing someone who wanted to invest in my education and wanted to invest in me, that inspired me. That made me want to perform and even out-perform people in my class and across the country. That *really* inspired me – seeing that someone cared about my education more than I did."

She said that her teachers "went above and beyond. They knew the power of connecting the curriculum to our lives – whether it was in history, math, English, or college prep class. Hands-on learning was important for them, because they knew we would be forced to critically think about problems and solutions to those problems. Even though I rarely ever took advantage of the opportunities, my teachers were readily available almost every evening for tutoring. And they were young and vibrant – still working towards accomplishing their own personal and professional goals, so it was like we were accomplishing our goals together. The best part about accomplishing goals together is that no one is the expert – we were all still learning and striving for excellence."

Jordan went on to communicate the important role mentorship played in her high school life. "Mentorship is *so* important," she asserted, "in schools where most of the students will go on to be first-generation college students. You don't know what you don't know and teachers can help to fill those gaps for parents when it comes to the college process, SATs, college applications, and personal statements."

Her teachers, and sometimes even their family members, served in mentorship roles in terms of Jordan's advocacy work.

"My tenth grade U.S. history teacher's mom, Mary Ann Livingston, is a professional speech writer and helped me draft my first fifteen-minute keynote that I gave before 6,000 youth. She is the reason why I can write speeches with such confidence and efficiency today. It was an honor having her take time out of her schedule to just help me succeed."

Overcoming Challenges

Jordan said that there have been definite challenges – and tradeoffs – involved in the work that she is doing.

Because she began her activist work in tenth grade, she had to make choices about how she wanted to spend her time and energy.

"My high school social life wasn't about going to football games, or going out and skating, or going to movies," she said. "It was working on a speech to open up at events for people like Hillary Clinton. And that was really cool, but there always comes a time when the pressure of it all just kind of gets to me."

She said that there have been times she has wondered if she made the right tradeoffs, but ultimately she has realized she would not have wanted to delay her environmental work until high school was over.

Still, she acknowledged that there was not always a comfortable place for her at the social table in high school.

She sometimes felt like she did not fit in – not because anyone was actively trying to shun her, but simply because "nobody really understood." When she tried to talk to her peers about an event she had held or a speaking engagement she found particularly energizing, even some of her closest friends at school were not able to relate. They had not yet had the sorts of experiences that Jordan had benefited from, and had a hard time understanding the ups and downs of the work she was striving to do.

"And I just didn't know who to talk to and I just wanted to be kind of normal. You know, like in Superman – he wants to be a regular person but it's hard for him, and Batman, too. So that's what I struggle with – wanting to be that person who just went to school and went home right after and did homework and then, you know, watched TV or whatever."

Yet because of her passion for her work, she knew that this kind of "normal" adolescence wasn't ever going to be hers. And eventually, she said she came to terms with that reality.

On the days when she feels less than motivated to work, Jordan said a reminder of her purpose grounds her and brings her back to what she needs to do.

There are times, or course, that she "just wants to chill."

"I just want to listen to music sometimes, or I just want to wake up and not do anything and not have to look at my calendar and see who I'm meeting with today, what speech I have to focus on, or what I have to fix on my website."

And yet, those moments don't last for long.

"There are times when I haven't really focused on a lot of work," she said.

But soon, she said she feels that familiar calling, whispering to her again and spurring her onward.

"I just feel the need to want to be busy," she shared, smiling knowingly. "I miss it. I want to be busy because I've found that this is my purpose; this is what I'm supposed to do. I can't thrive on just being regular."

On her Generation

While some adults might view Jordan's age as a disadvantage – something that she has to overcome in the work she is now doing – she actually views it as both an advantage and a tremendous responsibility.

She elaborated by saying, "I think that youth, kids from about – why not say three – from three to nineteen years old, I think that we are the most powerful people. Whether we're talking to our parents – convincing them to give us a car, buy us a toy that we want, or let us go to a party – we are persuasive. We can persuade politicians, parents, aunties, uncles, godparents, grandmothers; we have that magic to persuade them to do what we want. And I think it's our job to use it for good. Because when we speak, people listen."

Jordan also spoke about the characterization of young people as apathetic or slow to get involved in social justice work, saying she thinks that in most cases, young people who are apathetic are merely responding to the expectations established by the people – both young and old – around them.

"When you have low expectations for someone," she claimed, "of course they're going to play out, they're not going to perform. When you have high expectations – that's one of the things that I learned in school – when you have high expectations for us we'll rise to those expectations."

Jordan said that she has benefitted dramatically from having adults in her life who have held her to particularly high expectations.

"I think that from the beginning of my work everything that I have done has been because a teacher pushed me or just said simply that I could do it even when I didn't think I could," she said. "For instance, the first time that I ever spoke publicly was at an event where Hillary Clinton was speaking. I opened up for Hillary Clinton. My teacher had exaggerated to someone and said that I was this great public speaker and I'm like, 'Wait, I've never done this before.' It was a political fundraiser for Barack Obama. It was about a month before the 2008 election and it was the first carbon neutral political fundraiser in the nation. So it was an event in LA where the greenies, the celebrities, and people with money in LA were saying, 'We support Barack Obama and his energy and environment plan.' And the only reason I had the opportunity to speak at that event was because my teacher just put me in a position that I felt really awkward with and she knew that I could do it and I didn't know that I could do it until I did it."

She admitted that if her teacher had not created the opportunity for her, it might have been a long time before she recognized her strength as a public speaker. Instead of being in the limelight, she might have opted for the shadows.

When we asked Jordan what she wished her parents' generation knew about young people today, she smiled and eagerly shared her perspective on a question that she said she wished more adults would ask young people: "I think the most important thing adults need to know – just like they tell us all the time when we're in trouble – is that they were kids, too. They were kids too, so they had goals and dreams and they had these minds before, too. I think a lot of times you have adults who don't think about bringing young people into the conversation."

Jordan said she is sometimes frustrated when she attends conferences as an environmental activist and finds that conference organizers have positioned the youth tents in out-of-the-way areas, where they are less likely to get attention or conference traffic.

She said the experience always disappoints her, and she wishes that conference organizers would recognize that they are causing young people to feel unheard, unwanted, and even misunderstood.

She said her message to organizers of such events would be: "We want to be part of the conversation because when you were a kid, when you were a teenager, you also wanted to be a part of the conversation. So don't shut me out because I'm seventeen, eighteen, or nineteen years old. Bring me in and see what I have to offer. Because I do have something to offer, just like you have something to offer and you knew you had something to offer when you were my age."

She also said that in order for adults to connect with youth, the greatest thing they can do is seek such connections: "Knowing when you were a teenager, what did you like? How did you like to be talked to? How did you like to be talked with? And that's one of the most important things about connecting with anyone – finding the traits that are the same and knowing what makes us go '*Wow!*' Also, adults need to take an interest in what we don't like and how we don't like being talked down to."

The Promise of Technology

When she talked about technology and the potential it has to connect, educate and empower people, Jordan's face immediately lit up.

"I love social networking. I love Twitter. I love Facebook. I think that social networking has really opened up the world," she said.

She said that technology has helped her to connect with passionate young people who are just as interested in social issues as she is.

"I've met by accident so many youth from across the world who are doing amazing things and that also contributes to my motivation," she said. "When you see somebody thirteen years old debating with adults about education, that's inspiring to me. That keeps me going. I never think that I'm the only one doing this work, but when you see someone else and hear their story and see their videos, it's like, 'Wow, look at this.' I was in the same position five years ago, but it's still inspiring to know that you're not the only one and I think that social media has helped me. It's like a journal with different followers, people from all over the world and I just feel powerful, like I think anyone would, when I feel like I have this big audience."

Jordan talked about how technology energizes her personally, along with all the ways it is both fueling her generation and setting it apart from previous generations.

"Technology. That's what excites me. I hear a lot from adults about how they hate technology. I was sitting in class yesterday and our teacher was giving us a long lecture, while holding his iPhone, about how much he hates technology. Well, he can't hate it, because he's holding an iPhone. And he's talking about how he doesn't like our phones, and if he sees our phones he's going to do this, and he's giving us this long, negative lecture about technology." She shared another similar story from another recent class: "I was in a class recently and another teacher was telling us how she didn't want us to use our iPads to take notes and I was like, 'What? Why? What's the point of that?'"

Jordan believes that technology equips people, both young and old, with powerful tools, especially with regard to environmental justice: "There's this app where you can plant a tree, and it will remind you how many times to water it, based on what type of tree it is and where you live in the country, what region that you're in. There are apps that connect you with people all over the country. There are apps where you can look at the news when you're anywhere. I think technology is educating us and it's going to take us to the next level if we go with it and if we learn how to use it in the right way."

Defining Success

When asked how she defines success, Jordan recited her favorite quote from Maya Angelou: "People will forget what you said; people will forget what you did; but people will never forget how you made them feel."

Jordan then went on to share a personal anecdote about a memory from her grandmother's funeral when she was nine or ten years old.

She said she vividly remembers people getting up at the service and talking about how her grandmother made them feel. She elaborated, "People I had never seen in my life – and I was around this woman every day, every day she'd watched me – were all saying similar things about my grandma. And whether people knew her well or had had one conversation with her, they were all saying the same thing – she made me feel this way and I'm like, 'Wow, they don't even know her that well because I don't know them,' and yet they were all saying the same thing and I was like, 'Wow, I want to make sure that I inspire people, and not only inspire them, but inspire them into action.' And I think that, for me, is success. Success is not monetary; it's not anything materialistic. But it is about feelings and what you inspire in people."

Jordan shared that she is proud when someone remembers something she said in a speech – and even more proud when what they remember inspires them to live differently.

She went on to explain: "I keynoted at this conference in front of 6,000 kids and adults and teachers. It was the *International City of Los Angeles Youth Conference*, and there were 6,000 people, but it looked like a million people to me because I was on that stage, and kids from second to twelfth grade are screaming and I don't know if they can hear what I'm actually saying. But then I was at a meeting a month ago and a parent said, 'I remember your speech. You know, when you said to refuse plastic straws I told my wife we're never using plastic straws again.' So little things like that are what mean a lot to me. The achievements and the awards are very nice, but when someone tells me that they do something because I suggested they do it or I gave them that challenge, and they actually do it and listen and are inspired – that's what I'm most proud of."

Strengths, Weaknesses, and Challenges

Jordan said she is moved by working cooperatively and doing her part to encourage others. She stated that because of her interest in mentoring, she does not mind sharing responsibilities – or credit.

"I like working in a group and mentoring. I think that to me one of the biggest impacts in my life has been the mentors that I have met throughout the years – whether it's been someone I talk to every week or someone I just catch up with every three months. So mentoring is valuable to me. I make sure always with the projects I do, I make sure that there is someone who knows everything that I'm doing. Even if I am in charge of this program, they know what I'm doing because next year I might not be in this same place and I want someone else to be able to take over and carry on. I want the programs I create to be sustainable."

She also described her biggest weakness as trying to do too many things at once and acknowledged that she cannot "give 100 percent to every single project at the same time."

For Jordan, maintaining balance in her life has been, and continues to be, her biggest challenge.

She revealed, "One of the biggest reasons I think I didn't get accepted to Howard University was because I lacked balance in my life."

Too often, she said that her academic life has been the first thing she has sacrificed when working hard.

"When I was in high school I didn't focus on school as much as I should have," she reflected. "I focused on going to the board meetings and the speeches and traveling to this school and that school and I didn't focus on my academics. And what I used to say back then was, 'I'm focusing on my dream, my passion and what inspires me.' And it's okay to focus on your passion, but at that time I was seventeen years old and my job was school and so passion should have come second and school should have come first. So that was one of my biggest mistakes – to not have found that balance in my life – because when I was just focusing on the environmental work and wasn't focusing on school, I wasn't focusing on me. I wasn't focusing on my family and then everything went tumbling down."

Handling Criticism

Dealing with criticism seems to be something that Jordan does with ease.

She explained further, "I love people, I love people's opinions. I like to hear what people have to say."

She went on to share a specific story of a time when she was criticized in a very public forum, by a somewhat unlikely source: "I was in North Carolina at a US Green Building Council event. It was the organization's annual fundraiser and the keynote of the night was a senator who is on the environmental committee. I opened up the event and gave this inspiring speech and shared with the audience what youth are doing in the environmental movement and what they can do as well. And the senator got up there after I gave my speech and said, 'That's cute and all, but you're dreaming.'" Jordan shared that she was sitting in the front row and was in disbelief. She said his whole speech turned into a lecture about how she was in the clouds dreaming and it was nice to hear what she had to say, but none of it was really based in reality.

Afterward, organizers of the event tried to reassure her, fearing she would be devastated by the legislator's potentially soul-stripping words.

But Jordan made it clear she was not distraught by what happened.

Instead, she embraced the experience as best she could, recognizing it as a valuable learning experience.

"It's okay. It was great for me to learn," she said evenly.

She said she also has learned how different people – and different regions of the country – are at different stages of environmental understanding.

"I mean, I'm from California. I'm from LA, one of the greenest places and we say it's not green, but when you travel to places where people are like, "Global warming? Environment?' And you assume that everyone else is doing things like recycling. And I'm saying, 'Okay, recycling is baby steps. That's the smallest thing that you could ever do.' And some people are saying, 'Recycling? Don't even do it.' And people don't even recycle."

And those different stages of understanding make for some challenging conversations – conversations where courage and honesty are musts.

"I think criticism is good, especially for an activist in any field because you learn that people don't think the same way as you and so it makes you reflect on your own practices," she said.

In the case of the critical senator, Jordan said she has thought a lot about whether she might have done anything differently, and whether she made the most of the opportunity she had to influence him and others in the room at the time.

"I had to go back after that and say, 'Okay, what could I have said that would have appealed to him? Could I have talked about environmental economics or business?' Criticism forces you to appeal to your critics, which is what I should be doing as a public speaker anyway – appealing to my audience. And so I think the criticism, especially that, was interesting. It was good for me to learn from that experience."

Charting her Future

Jordan, like all of the young people featured in this book, is an individual whose future is wide open to her. Her intelligence, passion, hard work, and the connections she has already built are likely to help her create a variety of opportunities for herself and others.

But whatever she does, she said she knows that finishing college is at the top of her priority list.

"Higher education is definitely important to me," she said. "My whole story is 'education is empowerment,' so I mean, education for me is definitely a lifelong thing."

She said her parents have helped her to see the value of college, even though they did not complete college themselves.

"My dad went to UCLA for two years and then left to go to the military for the next twenty years of his life and I think my mom has always wanted to go to college. She was about to go back to school right before she had my baby sister," Jordan recalled. "I think that education is definitely expensive, but ignorance is way more expensive. And in college you have to learn these tools. Not just tools to go into the workforce, but tools of life – how to work with people, how to talk to professors – you learn way more than just what is in the books in college."

Although Jordan went to a public high school with a strong emphasis on sending students directly to four-year colleges and universities, she made the personal decision to attend a community college – a choice that has opened up a lot of opportunities for her.

She chose to go to Santa Monica College just before she was scheduled to begin a four-year college career in Vermont. She said she realized that if she left for Vermont, she would be turning her back on her dream of attending Howard University – a school where she applied but was not admitted.

"I want to transfer to Howard University in Washington DC," she said. "It's always been my dream school and when I wasn't accepted, that was like the craziest time. I'm happy that I made this decision. I wasn't happy when I first went to Santa Monica. I wasn't excited to go at all because I went to a college prep high school, so they didn't teach us about community college. But I really think that I've learned a lot about myself in the last year and a half."

While focusing on her college work, Jordan also said she wants to concentrate on creating sustainability in the work that she has already done.

"I'm making sure the projects I've done can be carried on by others," she shared. "I organized a green prom before at my high school, but I need to make sure I have something on my website that teaches someone how to have a green prom as well. I also need to put something up that teaches how to do a *Rise Above Plastics* program. So just making sure that the projects I've done are sustainable and that anyone can easily go to my website and be able to say, 'OK, I have an idea for that and here's how we can get it done.'"

The theme of being a leader who educates others ran consistently throughout Jordan's interview.

This was in part because of the mentorship experiences she had with her teachers at her charter school – and also because she recognizes how different her life might be today if her family's only choice had been to send her to her neighborhood school, where so few students graduate from high school, much less attend college.

When we asked her what her plans for the future were, she told us, "I want to reform the public education system in the United States. That's what I want to do. I don't know how big I want to go or how small, but I want to reform. I want to be one of the people who reform the public education system."

Jordan then went on to clarify, "Reform means that kids will be educated, that they'll want to come to school and they'll be inspired to come to school. They'll be inspired by their teachers, they'll be mentored by the teachers – and the teachers will be inspired by the students. The administrators will be inspired to give the teachers what they need so that they can give the students what they need. It's also important that kids are not just graduating from high school, but going to college, and wanting to go to college and being able to go to college if they want to."

Update

We interviewed Jordan for this book in the early fall of 2011. The following spring, she teamed up with *5 Gyres* and helped facilitate a youth conference at the American Embassy School in Delhi, India. Working with both elementary and middle school students, Jordan said she "equipped them with the skills to lead their own service projects in their schools and throughout India. Target cities of our project included Delhi, Chennai, and Bombay. It was amazing traveling and meeting with passionate young people. The younger they were, the more fired up and passionate they were about solving global issues. This is one trait I hope to never lose – the passion for social justice."

In February of this year, we received the following update from Jordan: "Over the past two years, I've taken a break from speaking at conferences and schools and began working on projects with non-profit organizations like *Surfrider Foundation, 5 Gyres,* and *Greening Forward.* After speaking at forums all over the world and meeting youth leaders working on other social issues, I began to see a common thread. It's rare that students are keynoting conferences, lobbying in their local and federal government offices, and sitting at the decision table for organizations. Over the years, I've been looked at as exceptional for sitting at the table or being the youngest to not only speak at an event, but to even receive an invitation to attend the event in the first place. I am great – I am. But there is nothing exceptional about me. I was given the opportunity to lead at a young age, and I took it. I was given the opportunity to amplify my voice at a young age, and I did. I am now focused on equipping young people with the tools they need to succeed as young leaders. Whether it is hosting public speaking workshops in schools, confidence building exercises at conferences, or teaching others about the power of service, it is my responsibility to ensure that more young people in underserved communities are given the tools to utilize their voices for social justice. That's what I'm working on now, with student-centered education reform initiatives like *Student Voice,* and that is what my brand will be focused on over the next few years – Movement Building."

CHAPTER THREE

MARYPAT HECTOR
ATLANTA, GEORGIA
Youth in Action and
National Action Network's Youth Move
Early Fall 2011, Age 13

"Stay true to your organization and to the vision that you have for your organization – that's success for me. Not how much money you make or how many suits and ties you wear, but staying true to yourself."

In a recent Facebook post, MaryPat announced her plan to run for U.S. President in the year 2044. She then went on to say that she has a lot of work to do to prepare for that campaign bid.

At first glance, her resume and experience up to this point in her life rival those of most people two or three times her age. And yet when asked to describe her work in a single sentence, MaryPat stated, "I'm trying to get a group of kids with me to try to change the world one project at a time."

For MaryPat, it really is as simple and as complicated as that single quest. When we asked her what this kind of work looked like, she explained: "It is happening one child at a time, one city at a time." MaryPat travels around the country in order not only to get more youth involved in her own non-profit organization, *Youth in Action,* but also more generally to "get them motivated and let them know that in order to change this world, you have to realize that if you don't like something then you have to do something about it. No matter how young you are, dream big and don't let anyone tell you that you can't do something."

When MaryPat was nine years old, she wrote a play entitled *Easy Street Ain't So Easy.* "The play," MaryPat explained, "was based on a true story about my friend who was going through issues at home and ever since she shared with me what she was going through, I knew that I not only wanted to stop child abuse, but also wanted to get involved in different issues affecting young people." And from focusing on recycling efforts, to gang and gun violence, to voter turnout, MaryPat has certainly been involved.

When she was ten years old, MaryPat founded the non-profit organization *Youth in Action.* "If you were to travel to Stone Mountain, Georgia," MaryPat explained, "there are no recreation centers within walking distance of where we live and go to school. Most adults work late and kids get bored, and so they start to turn to violence as the answer." MaryPat said she saw this repeated violence in her community and wanted to have a sit-in to raise awareness about what she saw. "I wanted to have a sit-in to stop violence in my community and I wanted to have thirty or forty kids sit outside and sleep outside for about three days and that's how *Youth In Action* was founded." Some of her earliest projects involved a violence awareness campaign and the institution of a recycling program in her hometown of Stone Mountain.

Youth in Action has become one of the fastest growing youth-led organizations in the nation. The networks work to kick off community service projects that address specific community issues, like problems with youth violence, child abuse, and homelessness.

As the Youth Director for the National Action Network's (NAN's) *Youth Move*, MaryPat also speaks across the country, educating youth on a variety of issues. Through her varied work, she travels about 4,000 miles a month, speaking at K-12 schools and colleges, conferences, women's events, and other gatherings.

She shared that for the most part, she has had very positive experiences with getting other young people involved with *Youth in Action*. "They actually like it," she smiled. "They enjoy the fact that they are changing the world in meaningful ways." She said that she believes what drives other young people to be involved in *Youth in Action* mirrors why she herself founded the organization. "People who actually care about the movement," she said, "and care about changing the world one project at a time, are driven by knowing in their hearts that they can change the world no matter what anybody says."

MaryPat did disclose, however, that she has had some experience with people who used her organization for her contacts and "basically took advantage of what I was doing and what *Youth in Action* was doing." She said that, although rare, these instances did challenge – but not deter – her and her work.

Motivation, Support, and Role Models

MaryPat is motivated largely by the injustices she sees in the world around her. She has spent time following court cases and organizing rallies and community events for causes she sees as important within the social justice realm, and frequently does her own research to try to get to the bottom of widely reported cases, including the Troy Davis case.

"I see a lot of things that I don't feel are right in the world," she shared. "Some people are different. I went to the Troy Davis trial the other day and seven people recanted and said he was innocent and he didn't do it. And some people say that he wasn't innocent and he did murder the police officer. But I guess what really motivates me is when people don't really look into something all the way and they don't see it through and they just make a big decision. And that could be not only with the government – I'm okay with my government – but with anything."

She said what is important is not necessarily the conclusion you reach in the end as much as the valuing of truth and justice along the way.

"But as a young person, what motivates me is to let adults know that we can truly change the world, we do have a voice, and our generation is not going downhill."

She went on to talk about how the media portrays her generation: "I see on the news where teenagers are doing crazy things and I would like to see for once the media show what positive youth are doing – and that's why I love this book you're writing– to show what positive youth are doing. And that's it. That's what motivates me."

She said she is never tempted to turn her back on her work.

"You know, I never have one of those days where I'm like, 'You know what? Forget this.' Because if so many people gave up their work, where would we be today if they just threw it all away? And sometimes I do have those days when I – not that I don't want to work, because I always want to work – realize that it's up to me. It's up to me if I want to work. Sometimes my mom and my god-sister are just like, 'Mary, just go out, have fun.' And I'm like, 'No, I want to work.' Work is fun to me. You know, changing the world and getting more kids involved in the movement. That's fun. Sometimes my mom and god-sister push me to be a normal teenager. That's what they want for me, but that's not what I want for myself. And so they support me in what I want for myself as well."

In her personal life, MaryPat has many role models who she can call on for support, including all of her aunts, her mom, and her dad. She said she "looks up to them a lot because I think to myself sometimes, 'Who am I not to be great if they've given me all these opportunities? If they've invested so much time and money in me, everybody, who am I not to be great?' I have the opportunity – it's right in front of me – so I have to take it. I have to take that chance."

MaryPat also credits her success to others she looks to for support and motivation.

"I look up to people like Tamika Mallory," MaryPat said, referring to a NAN leader. "She got involved in the movement a good twenty years ago and she's like – what – thirty-two now, and so she got started at a very young age." MaryPat also looks up to Oprah because "as a woman, I just love that people aren't stuck on the limitations of being female – I love that women can change the world as well." MaryPat admires the fact that Oprah got started in her work at a young age as a journalist. MaryPat said that she has had aspirations of becoming a journalist herself and so she "just looks up to Oprah."

After talking about Oprah, she smiled, "I also look up to my mommy."

MaryPat also looks up to people "like Russell Simmons because he always just wants kids to be out there and he's always helping them in so many ways and I write for his blog right now and you can look at all of my political issues and how I feel about so many things."

She has a great deal of respect for another mentor who has helped to advance her work directly, the Rev. Al Sharpton.

"He's been so good to me and my organization. Honestly, without his help I could not be where I am today. That day I did that sit-in when I had thirty to forty kids outside sleeping in these tents on Memorial Drive, you know, adults didn't show up. We thought that adults really didn't care and so I called in to Reverend Sharpton's show and I said, 'Look here, Reverend Sharpton,' I said, 'Look here. We slept out here on Memorial Drive for two to three days, we haven't taken showers in days because we're tired of the violence in our communities and we're finally standing up and adults aren't helping us, so we need your help.' And what is Reverend Sharpton supposed to say on his live radio show but 'Sure, why not?' So about thirty minutes later he had his Atlanta chapter of *National Action Network* (NAN) come out and he was moving fast to mobilize people to help us. Ever since then, NAN and *Youth in Action* have partnered in a way and without that help and without him letting me meet people from the NAACP (*National Association for the Advancement of Colored People*) and the SCLC (*Southern Christian Leadership Conference*) and other organizations – big organizations – I don't know what I would do. I wouldn't be as far as I am today without that help."

NAN works closely with MaryPat and the relationship is likely to continue to be important in the future. The organization's emphasis on social justice and activism is a natural fit for MaryPat. She has worked with initiatives in areas including education, access to legal justice, and anti-violence measures, and appreciates the way the group responds quickly to the big news stories of the day, as well as ongoing events and issues.

The blogging she does is an important outlet – and also a way for her to learn more about how others view her ideas. She appreciates the immediacy of blogging and the way that she can quickly communicate with sizable groups of people. And at times she has been challenged by the responses she has received.

"Not too long ago I wrote a blog post entitled *Parents Are Helping the Youth to Die* and I just got so much negative feedback from that particular blog, and I don't understand how so many adults were just like, 'Well, you don't know.' And you know what, I do know! And some of these adults were complaining about the music many young people listen to. And my message to them was simply, 'You know, who produces this music that you all hate so much? Why don't you all boycott this? Who gives us the money – who gives young people the money for those tight pants that you hate so much or those shorts or those sagging jeans that everyone just hates?' And that's what I was pretty much saying in my blog, you know, that adults – not all adults, some people thought I was talking about all adults and all parents and that's not what I was saying – I was saying for the adults that do say that the youth are killing America and that the youth are so violent, you know, who are the ones letting their kids watch violent TV shows and movies at such a young age? And they're seeing so much violence that they're getting immune to it."

MaryPat said she recognizes that her own brother is heavily influenced by what he sees in the media. The effects, she acknowledged, are both good and bad.

"My brother, Mason, is five years old and he'll sit in the kitchen and watch Batman cartoons and say, 'I want to be Batman. I want to be a superhero.' But that can be good in two ways: Mason knows that he's a superhero and that I'm – well, he calls me a superhero, too, because I change the world and I help people – but I try to let Mason know that superheroes don't always fight. Gandhi didn't fight, but he was a superhero because he did change the world in a peaceful way and I try to let him know that superheroes can change the world, but not always fight all the time and I try to let him know that he can help people like superheroes do."

She said that the violent, overly sexualized elements within the media will not change unless both adults and young people work together.

"If adults really want change and kids really want change, then we need to work together as one country, as one nation, and just say enough is enough."

On her Age

MaryPat cited being taken seriously at such a young age as one of the biggest challenges that she faces in her work. She revealed that "sometimes adults do not take me seriously because I'm still a child – I'm thirteen years old. I started this activist work when I was nine years old. And I see a lot of adults not believing that kids can change the world one project at a time and not expanding their minds and realizing that. I mean, we know every fight's not our fight, but we truly can change the world."

On one occasion, MaryPat said she walked up to a senator at an event, introduced herself, and shared the work she was doing with *Youth in Action.* MaryPat said "although he seemed interested at the time, it was like he didn't really care. Then, not too long after that I saw him talking to an adult about the exact same issue I was speaking with him about and he seemed ready to write her a check and I was thinking, 'How does she know what we need? How does she know what we want? She doesn't see what I see when I go to school or when I hang out with my friends. How does she know?' And that's just what I felt – that a lot of adults forget what it's like to be a teenager. They were once teenagers, but times have changed and that's when adults don't believe in kids and don't have hope and see our drive and passion."

Despite some age-related challenges, she does feel that her age is an advantage.

"I'm talking to adults who are down with the youth movement, who understand that even though they were young a long time ago, it was the youth that did change the world and that did have a collective voice that sparked the movement." She said that another disadvantage of her age is when "people think that kids need to just be kids and they think that kids can't change the world and they think it's all in adults' hands. But we are all people and we can all change the world in a way."

MaryPat went on to state how important she believes peer-to-peer interactions among young people are to her work. "When peers talk to peers – that's when they really talk," she expanded. "When we talk to adults, it's like we can't say everything we want to say. It might be offensive or sometimes it's just that we feel that adults won't understand." Yet, she countered, if young people feel that adults are truly interested in what youth have to say, then the young people are more likely to open up and share their ideas.

On Technology and Social Networking

"Facebook is awesome," MaryPat enthused. "That's how I've started so many chapters of *Youth in Action* in these different cities – through Facebook. I think it's amazing how fast information travels. When I post something on Facebook, people see what we're doing and they want to be a part of it. So I thank God for Facebook, because without Facebook I wouldn't have as many chapters of *Youth in Action* as I do now." That being said, MaryPat does feel that she could still do her work without social media and other technological resources. "I mean, if Gandhi could do it without social networking," she smiled, "I know I can."

Mistakes, Criticism, and Achievements

One of MaryPat's proudest moments was when she received a proclamation from President Obama. "That would have to be one of the best days of my life," she shared. "I couldn't even speak. When they handed me the paper that said Barack Obama's name on it, well, that right there was history in and of itself and now that MaryPat's name is right there next to his name on this paper with this award-type badge thing, I was just like, 'Yes, I have made it. He knows who I am.' Well, I know he doesn't know who I am like that, but it was still so exciting for me. That was a community service award."

She spoke at length of the moment when she found out she was the recipient of the President's honor: "I guess it was planned; they did it to me on purpose. I was in a board meeting and my board members stopped the meeting and I'm like, 'Oh, they just stopped my board meeting!' I was a little upset at the time, you know, because we were talking about *Youth in Action* and they stopped my board meeting and for a second I was like, 'Why are you all stopping my board meeting?' and my mom was like, 'Just shhhh!' And I was like, 'Mom, they stopped my board meeting!' and I was so upset at the fact they stopped my board meeting and then they pulled out this paper – this long sheet of paper – and they read it out loud and then they said it was from President Obama and they gave me my award and I was just happy. And then I was like, 'Yeah! They stopped my board meeting!'"

MaryPat said that, up to this point in time, she does not feel like she's made any really large mistakes in her work, except for right around the time of *Youth in Action's* founding. She shared that she "tried to force everybody to get involved. I told them, 'You know, you've got to change the world, you have to do this.'" She said now she understands that a lot of people don't see or share her vision and that that is okay: "Some people don't understand what I'm doing and I can't force it on anybody. And I know that now because I've grown up over the years and I've learned that everyone is different."

Because she sees her work as her art, she sometimes has a hard time handling criticism from others. "I'm one of those artsy people who's like, 'It's my artwork. Who are you all to change my art?'" she said. "But I mean, it depends on what kind of criticism it is. You know, sometimes I have those days where I'm writing on my blog and writing my stories and my mom asks me why I'm writing something or saying something a certain way and I'm like, 'Mom, it's the way I feel. *Global Grind* and other blogs and online news outlets want me to write for them because of how I feel.' And that's why I didn't understand when people were criticizing the recent blog post I mentioned earlier. I felt that I was just expressing my viewpoints and I didn't think people should have criticized me for that. But how I take criticism? It just depends on what kind of day it is and how I'm feeling. I think that happens for everybody, it depends on what kind of day it is for them and how they might feel about the topic I wrote about or what I'm talking about."

MaryPat elaborated on the experience with her recent blog post a bit further, and said it has been a learning experience: "At the time I felt that it was just a blog post about how I was feeling at that particular time." She said that she was confident in her opinion because the topic, youth violence, was something that she had been writing about, researching, and speaking on for quite some time. She said that even though a lot of people would not have written the blog post in the way that she did, she wrote it because "What am I afraid of? I'm not afraid of anything. I just couldn't believe that I was getting so much negative feedback from adults. They just did not understand what I was saying and they just weren't willing to open up their eyes and realize that they do have a part to play in the situation. And it was adults who were talking about how negative certain things are on television. And I told them, 'You know, you still have cable. You still listen to the radio. You're still tuning into that negative radio station that you're complaining about. You're supporting this. You'll still flip it on to the *Bad Girls Club* and what not. If you really want to stop this, then you can.' And it's about the kids, too. Who's buying this music for the kids? Who's teaching them and raising them? And even if you don't have any kids, don't be afraid to mentor someone else's child because not everyone can really take care of their own children. But if you can, I think it's everybody's responsibility on this planet to make sure everyone strives to be their very best that they can be, so yes. Like Gandhi said – you must be the change that you want to see in this world. It's everybody, we're one. I think that we should all help each other."

While processing criticism differently on different days, MaryPat does seem to have a strong understanding of her assets and weaknesses.

"One of my biggest strengths would be talking. I talk a lot. I also think that I'm really good at just motivating people to get up and do something."

"My greatest weakness would have to be how I deal with people who talk about wanting to change the world and then are not doing anything at all. Sometimes, I'll go up to people who are talking about a certain issue and just say, 'What are you doing in your community to stop that?' So I know that's my weakness – asking people, 'Well, what are you doing? How are you changing the world?' And I'm not trying to be mean or disrespectful, but I just feel it's important to ask people these questions. I know a lot of people think that I'm stepping out of a child's place when I do this, so that would have to be a weakness of mine. My mom's like, 'You just can't ask everybody what are they doing for themselves,' but I do and I guess that would have to be a weakness of mine."

When asked how she finds balance in her busy life, she responded without hesitation, "It would have to be my mommy. My mommy balances me, and so does my god-sister. They both balance me out a lot. They remind me, 'Mar, you're only thirteen. Just remember you've got a lot ahead of you.' They keep me focused. Sometimes when I fall off they ask me what I'm trying to do and they just roll me right back on track because this is my vision and I am going to see it through. So it's my mom and my god-sister Maya who keep me balanced the most."

On Connecting with her Generation

MaryPat had quite a few ideas regarding what it takes to connect to her generation: "This generation has a mind of its own. It seems that this generation's not afraid to just speak out and be heard. If they're not getting attention in a positive way, they're getting it in a negative way and I think we just need to push them towards that positive way, because they are going to speak out one way or another. And parents need to allow their children – like I said before – to get their feet wet now before they make that big decision about what they want to do when they get older. And let their kids know that they can dream big and they don't have to wait to be great. They can change the world now. That's my saying. I say it all the time – 'Dream big. You don't have to wait to be great' – so you've heard that before. That's my saying."

She went on to say that she believes honesty is vital when adults are trying to connect with young people: "I mean, if you're honest with a young person, please believe me, they'll be honest with you and sometimes you'll just be taken aback by the stuff that they're talking about because sometimes I'm even taken aback by some of the stuff that young people nowadays will say. Sometimes I'm like, "Ahh, you're only sixteen.' But I'm thirteen. So you know, just be honest with us. We need that."

She said the most important thing that young people need from the adults in their lives is time. "I've always seen this," she expanded. "Adults say, 'Here's money to do this.' A kid says, 'I want to go shopping.' And her mom is like, 'Here's the money to go shopping.' Many parents buy time and they waste time, but they don't spend time. They don't spend time with their kids and I think that kids need time. There are a lot of things going on in our generation now and many parents aren't really spending time with their kids. Well, not all parents are doing this – I mean, I spend time with my mom all the time – but some parents need to spend more time with their kids instead of buying time with their kids, because we really need our parents' time."

MaryPat believes that change-seekers are what excite her generation the most: "People who aren't afraid to speak up and speak out and get loud and say we want to be heard – that's what I think excites my generation."

Defining Success

MaryPat singularly defines individual success as being true to your vision and what you need to do to fulfill your dreams and goals.

"Some people say, 'Well, I want to be a pianist.' Great. Be the best pianist you can be. Some people want to be schoolteachers. Be the best schoolteacher you can be. Think outside of the box and you'll be successful. Doing what you do best and doing it to the best of your ability and being great at it – that's success to me."

In terms of defining success for an organization, MaryPat talked quite a bit about authenticity and "staying true to the reason why you started your organization in the first place." She said that it is important to "never change, never fall out. I know sometimes organizations fall out due to money issues. They get so caught up in the money and the fame and fortune and they're not staying true to the reason why they actually founded their organization in the first place. So staying true to your organization and staying true to the vision that you have for your organization – that's success for me. Not how much money you make or how many suits and ties you wear, but staying true to yourself and your organization's vision."

Going forward, she said the biggest needs of her organization have to do with funding. "I mean, honestly speaking, I have hundreds and hundreds of youth in my organization," she explained. "This is a youth-led organization. When I get older, I hope to give my organization to a young person, because as I said earlier, to be successful as an organization, I want my vision to stay the exact same as it has been. But our biggest need would have to do with funding. You know, we travel a lot, opening up new chapters and being involved with projects throughout the country. I travel to NYC and South Carolina and North Carolina and Detroit and Chicago and I'm going back and forth, back and forth, and I even take some youth with me from the different organizations, other presidents, so funding is an issue. Also, every year each chapter focuses on a national initiative. Like right now we're focusing on the voting campaign and also shaking off violence. I've been leading the *Shake Off Violence* campaign for three years, but it feels like five years that I've been doing this, like I have gray hairs in my head. But, that's what we need. Funds. And help and support. We need help and support from a lot more people and if we had that help and support, well... That's what we need."

MaryPat said that the advice she'd give to a middle school student interested in activism work is simple: "Do it. Just do it. Just go ahead, don't be afraid. People are going to tell you a lot of things. People are going to tell you that you're just a child; people are going to tell you that you're just doing this for no reason; people are going to tell you all kinds of things. And there will be times when things don't happen as fast or as quickly as you want them to. Believe me. I know. And a lot of people know, but just do it and stay true to it and just never give up and it will happen. It will happen more quickly if you do start at a younger age. I know that for a fact."

Looking Toward her Future

"I want to go to college. I know I do. People who say they don't want to go to college for that college experience, they're lying to you. I want that college experience. I'm home schooled. I want to – I want to go to Georgia State University or Colgate University or Spellman College. I just want to go to college to get that feeling and also I want to be in politics and I know – well, you don't always have to go to college to be in politics – but I want to go to college to be in politics and I'm working on that now. I'm still getting my feet wet to see what I want to do. You know, I'm thirteen. I do so much in the community, working on different issues and projects, but I'm still trying to figure out what I want to major in. I've got about two more years to figure out what I want to do because I'm in ninth grade now but I know that college definitely does fit into my plans and I've gotten so many scholarships already. So who am I not to go ahead and go to college, why not try it out?"

"My plans for the future would have to be making *Youth in Action* worldwide and also I guess, in a way, changing the world one project at a time, or changing the world in my own way. That would have to be it."

MaryPat noted that in ten years, "I will still be the founder of *Youth in Action*, but I will not be the national president anymore. So, I'm thinking about how I can be involved in the leadership of other organizations, such as *National Action Network*, and also how I can just keep my vision as a person true to myself and just change the world, I guess, with other organizations and sometimes not just with other organizations but just by myself."

When we asked MaryPat where she sees herself in twenty years, she seemed a little baffled: "Twenty years from now? Gosh! I'll be what, thirty-three, going on thirty-four? I can't even picture myself at thirty-three, I can't. I can't see myself being that old. I don't know what I'll do, but I do know that I still want to help out with some of my family businesses. All my aunts and uncles work and so I want to help out with some family businesses that we have. I don't think I'll have kids at the age of thirty-three. I'll be too busy. Maybe when I'm thirty-eight or thirty-nine, before I get too old to have kids, I'll have kids and will just pour all the stuff that I was given, all the knowledge, into my kids and let them know that I'll be behind them 100 percent, just like my mom was for me – and like my uncles and aunts and my dad were."

MaryPat recognizes some of the geographic advantages she has had living in the Atlanta area, and hopes to use these going forward.

"I grew up in Atlanta, Georgia. And in some ways it's hard being an activist in Atlanta, Georgia, because we see people like Bernice King and the Abernathy family and we see these people walking up and down the street every day. It's like we're spoiled because we are so used to seeing these public figures around. Like when we go to NYC, people are like, 'You know the King family? You know Bernice King? You see Mayor Kasim Reed eating lunch with college students at the Waffle House?' And I'm like, 'Yeah, I'm just used to it.' I grew up in Atlanta and it's not hard. Well, everything in life is hard, but I didn't grow up with this hard life that I could talk about in a rap song or anything, but hey, I mean certain things I did were hard, getting people involved, but other than that, what can I say? I grew up in Atlanta. I'm trying to make change in Atlanta."

When we asked MaryPat if there was anything else she wanted to share with us, she smiled, "I don't think so. I pretty much poured everything out in this interview."

Update

We spent quite a bit of time with MaryPat during the later part of 2011. We interviewed her for this book, showed up to support her at community rallies and events, and followed her accomplishments closely in the media. If nothing else, the rapid-fire pace of her life reminds us that youth is fleeting. In late 2012, MaryPat was recognized by Ebony Magazine as one of *Ebony's Power 11*. She was recognized this same year by McDonald's as a *365 Honoree* for her youth empowerment work. She was also named as *2012's Youth of the Year* by the DeKalb chapter of the 100 Black Men of America and was honored with the *Drum Major for Justice Award 2012* from SCLC/Women's Organizational Movement for Empowerment Now. She is, clearly, on her way.

CHAPTER FOUR

MAX WALLACK
NATICK, MASSACHUSETTS
Puzzles to Remember

Late Fall 2011, Age 15

"I've really always lived by this motto: If you have the ability to help others, you have the responsibility to do so."

We learned about Max and his work through MaryPat Hector. During MaryPat's own interview, she talked quite a bit about Max. "You've just got to talk to this kid," she implored us. "He's doing some amazing work. We're really different, but you just have to talk to him. I think he'd be a great addition to the book." Her glowing recommendation led us to contact him and, after a brief initial talk and some background research on the work he has done, the decision to include him became an obvious one.

Among some other impressive accomplishments, Max is the founder of a non-profit organization called *Puzzles to Remember.*

Max described his organization like this: "We collect puzzles and distribute them to facilities that care for Alzheimer's and dementia patients. All together, we've collected 8,315 puzzles and distributed them to almost 900 locations across the U.S. and Canada and Mexico."

Max founded *Puzzles to Remember* in 2008, and in 2010, Springbok Puzzles came out with a line of Alzheimer's puzzles that Max worked to help develop. What makes these puzzles special, Max said, is that they are easier for Alzheimer's patients to complete because they feature a small number of big pieces along with colorful and reminiscent scenes that are appealing to older people with Alzheimer's.

When we asked Max how he first got involved with this work, he shared that he lives by the motto that if you have the ability to help others, you have the responsibility to do so.

He also had a personal reason for wanting to help the Alzheimer's community – his connection with his great grandmother.

Max's relationship with his great grandmother, Gertrude, sparked his interest in creating and donating puzzles to elderly people with Alzheimer's. From the time he was six until he was ten, Max spent a lot of time with his great grandmother, who suffered from the disease. She lived with his family, and he was quite close to her. Toward the end of her life, Max would visit her at her nursing home.

During his visits, Max noticed a lot of patients doing jigsaw puzzles, and he observed that while doing the puzzles, the patients seemed significantly less agitated than they were when engaged in other activities.

Max became curious about puzzles, why they worked, and their benefits. His work took off from there: "When I was eleven, I started researching about jigsaw puzzles and was seeing that they had beneficial effects on Alzheimer's patients, and, when I was twelve, I started collecting these puzzles, mostly from manufacturers. Then, I started reaching out to the general public." Not long after, *Puzzles to Remember* was founded.

When he is in an area with a nursing home that serves Alzheimer's patients, Max still "usually tries to go to that facility and deliver the puzzles, and, when I'm there, I'm sometimes able to work the puzzles with the patients. Seeing their faces makes me so happy, and, basically, they're always very thankful. I get positive reactions all the time."

Max said he believes the puzzles enrich the lives of Alzheimer's patients, providing them with a greater sense of dignity, while also challenging and entertaining them.

"I feel there was a dearth of puzzles that were available to Alzheimer's patients before these puzzles came out because even though a lot of people in day care and assisted living can do the 350-piece puzzles, a lot of Alzheimer's patients can't do those puzzles." He noted that most of the puzzles that were available were store-bought, were often juvenile in subject matter, and that patients "felt they're too old for those puzzles and they think of them as children's puzzles – they don't want to do those. So, I felt that that dearth of available puzzles was a really big obstacle. The puzzles we've created with Springbok Puzzles have been so helpful in filling that gap."

Max's work isn't limited to his *Puzzles to Remember* organization, although he shared with us that the same mantra that guides that work steers his other projects, too.

He explained: "When I was six, my family purchased a new mini-van and my great-grandmother was having a lot of trouble getting into that mini-van."

Max described how he noticed the challenges his great grandmother faced and figured out ways to help. "And so I designed for her a special step to help her get into that minivan. Then, when I was seven, I realized that she was having a lot of trouble standing up in department stores. She liked going shopping, but she couldn't really go as much because she needed to stand a lot more, and she really couldn't do that. So I designed her a special cane with a seat attached to it called the *Walk Away Cane*."

Max's family served as inspiration for other projects as well.

He explained that when he was twelve years old, he "started designing a special cushion called the carpal tunnel cushion for my grandmother who had carpal tunnel syndrome." When he was twelve, he also designed a contraption called the *home dome*. The inspiration for this project came six years earlier. His earlier invention, the *great-granny booster step*, won him an award and a trip to Chicago to accept this award. On the way to the awards ceremony, his family got lost in the city. Max remembered seeing a lot of homeless people sleeping in garbage bags and boxes. He recalled, "I really felt I should help them. When I was twelve, I realized that a good way to help them would be making a shelter for them out of recycled materials." Thus, his invention, the *home dome,* came to be.

The *home dome* is not currently manufactured or marketed. But Max doesn't seem to allow the project's shortcomings to bother him. Instead, he was able to talk about what he learned from the project, and then go on to talk about other work that is meaningful to him. Sometimes, he said, you can learn just as much from a project that seems unsuccessful as from one that is viewed by others as successful.

An Early Start

When Max was just four years old, he was accepted into a program called Davidson Young Scholars. He described this experience as a motivating factor in his life: "When I was there I met the founder, Jan Davidson, and a lot of other people. Mrs. Davidson gave a speech and said if you have the ability to help others you have the responsibility to do so. I really got motivated by that, and that's what I've been trying to do."

Max also talked about his belief in micro-philanthropy, which he described by saying, "basically, if everyone can just do a little bit we can really make a big difference."

The micro-philanthropy movement is structured to offer people opportunities to give in targeted ways to specific projects, instead of donating to large organizations, where the results of individual giving might be more difficult to see or appreciate.

The emphasis of micro-philanthropy is on the notion that small gifts can make a large difference, and that donating is not something that should be left only to the most affluent among us. The focus is on a "love of humanity" instead of on strictly donating money. There also is more interaction between donors and organizations, and giving may include volunteering or mentoring, instead of primarily just financial donations.

When we asked Max about whether or not he feels his age impacts the work that he does, his response differed from that of many of the other youth we talked to. He had the following to say: "I don't really feel that age has that much to do with what one can accomplish. I think that having someone who's young do all these things just kind of makes other people feel inspired to do them themselves. I'm not sure if being young has actual direct benefits to the work that I do other than inspiring other people to do the work."

On his Generation

Max challenged the common notion of the media's portrayal of youth as apathetic. Conversely, Max shared his belief that he thinks many of his peers truly can improve their communities. He stated that if there is one thing that today's young people wish that their parents knew about his generation, it would be that "we really can help and we really can make a difference." In order for adults to effectively connect with youth, Max said, the adults should find a common, altruistic interest with the young people in their lives. And then they should get to work – together.

On Technology

Max uses technology in a variety of ways in his work. He feels that "social networking can really help get the word out about a project or idea and can help with getting a lot of other people involved." Max also blogs and serves as the editor for the *Alzheimer's Reading Room*, which is "one of the biggest sites for caregivers of Alzheimer's patients." Max feels that social networking and blogging can not only help get the word out about his work, but also can "help instill hope and techniques and be a really positive influence on caregivers of Alzheimer's patients."

He balanced these statements, however, by explaining that there are a lot of facets of his work that he is able to accomplish without social networking. There are times when face-to-face interactions are needed – and effective. For example, he said that he regularly speaks to people in Rotary clubs and other service organizations to let others know about *Puzzles to Remember*. He elaborated: "I'm still trying to get the word out without doing just social networking and blogging."

Strengths, Weaknesses, and Defining Success

Max defines personal success as "feeling that you've really helped someone and accomplished something to help the community."

For his organization, he defines success more specifically as "bringing these patients something that they can use to express themselves and help themselves and really make them happy for even an hour." He said that if patients can be happier, calmer, and less agitated – for even a short time – then that experience has the potential to change their entire day or even week. He elaborated, "And they might not even remember doing the puzzle after an hour, but they still feel that they did something, and they feel happy and accomplished that they did that. That's one of the biggest things that you can bring to an Alzheimer's patient because a lot of Alzheimer's patients no longer experience feelings of success and many are actually clinically depressed."

The ways Max defines success closely align with his own self-professed strength, which is "really being able to find a need and help people have that need met by either inventing something for them or supplying them with something that can really help them."

Max believes that "founding *Puzzles to Remember* and really having it grow so much is an amazing achievement, but also I feel very proud that I have had the opportunity to work in Boston University's Pharmacology and Experimental Therapeutics Lab, where I'm studying certain proteins and enzymes involved in Alzheimer's disease." He appreciates that he is able to help do research in the field of Alzheimer's and "really work with some brilliant, humble, and inspirational scientists." He feels this work "is something that not many people get to do and it's an amazing feeling."

When we asked Max about one of his weaknesses, he surprised us by shifting from talking about work to discussing his martial arts hobby: "I feel that my weakness is sort of unrelated to my work, but it is taekwondo. I really love doing taekwondo but it's very hard for me to do." He said that "I'm still a recommended black belt and you have to do a difficult physical endurance test. I had to do it three times before I could pass it. It was really, really challenging for me. Many academic subjects come easy to me, so this experience taught me to better understand students who are having a hard time academically, so that I can be more empathetic toward them."

Max was not able to point to any large mistake he feels he has made in work, but rather to many small mistakes along the way: "When I was building the prototypes of my inventions, I was always making little mistakes that I needed to correct in order to make the whole project better." He went on to say, however, that through repeated testing he was able to correct these mistakes.

Max does not feel that he has encountered much criticism in his work. Conversely, "I've found almost everyone very supportive and very helpful. I feel like when people really understand the work I'm doing and my philanthropy, most people are really helpful and giving." He said, "I don't really feel that anyone's questioned my work because nobody's really said to me, 'Oh, you couldn't have done all this great stuff.' They've looked at me and said, 'You've done all this stuff – that really inspires me to do more things, too.' I feel that people have very positive reactions when they hear about what I do."

Max also credits some supporters who have helped to make the work he's done possible: "MaryPat has been supportive; Bob DeMarco, the founder of the *Alzheimer's Reading Room* has been very supportive and helpful; and Carol Larkin, a Geriatric Care Manager, has been very helpful. I have also been inspired by my mentors at the Boston University Alzheimer's Research Center, Dr. Oiu and Dr. Zhu. They have always been very supportive of my work, and I've actually been helping them with their research. For coursework, I take all my academic classes at BU."

Looking Ahead

Max's vision for his future seems clear. He plans on majoring in neuroscience and then going to medical school. At the time of our first interview, Max said he was deciding between Boston University and Brown University. In ten years, he plans on being settled into his career as a geriatric psychiatrist. He elaborated: "I feel like in ten years I will have really helped a lot of Alzheimer's patients and I'll also have done a lot of research on the disease. In that way, I'll be able to help patients in not only the personal and emotional aspects of the disease, but also the more biological aspects." Max also aspires to help caregivers of Alzheimer's patients to deal with some of the emotional challenges they face.

As for *Puzzles to Remember*, he does anticipate some needs for the organization going forward. He noted that although he does receive a lot of puzzle donations, he will require help and financial support for distributing the puzzles. And although Max said he has the help of some great volunteers, he does still do a lot of the work on his own.

Concluding Thoughts

When we asked Max what advice he would give to a middle school student interested in pursuing non-profit work, his answer was succinct and profound, reflecting his micro-philanthropic orientation: "Every little bit helps."

When we asked Max if there was anything else he wanted to share with us, he volunteered the following: "I feel that another really important part of my contribution to society is working on research, because that's really the other half of what I'm doing." At the beginning of the summer of 2011, he was working with a cancer drug to see if it had any effect on the degradation of Amyloid beta, a protein implicated in Alzheimer's disease. He went on to talk about the fact that this trial "didn't really work out that well because the drug was really hard to develop. We are considering moving on to other cancer drugs that are in that same family. And right now, I'm working on seeing if cerebral spinal fluid and serum have the same levels of different enzymes that are associated with Alzheimer's disease. This work could lead to a blood test to diagnose Alzheimer's disease at an early stage when treatment is more effective."

An unwavering sense of purpose, a desire to use his talents and intelligence to make the world around him a better place, and an unassuming nature despite success and accolades are just some of the qualities that we know will serve Max well in the future.

Update

We interviewed Max for this book in the fall of 2011. Since that time, he has graduated from high school. He is now a sixteen-year-old sophomore at Boston University and a Research Intern in the Molecular Psychiatry and Aging Laboratory in the Department of Pharmacology and Experimental Therapeutics at Boston University School of Medicine, where he volunteers about twenty hours a week during the school year and full-time during the summers. To date, *Puzzles to Remember* has distributed more than 19,720 puzzles to over 1,725 Alzheimer's caregiving facilities in all fifty states and numerous foreign countries. Max continues to be an editor for the *Alzheimer's Reading Room*, where he interacts with Alzheimer's caregivers around the world. Often, Max is asked questions about how to explain Alzheimer's disease to children. As a result, he is completing a manuscript for a book for children between the ages of four and nine, explaining Alzheimer's disease and, hopefully, providing children with some coping skills. He is currently looking for a publisher for his book.

Last year, Max was offered complimentary membership in the American Association for Geriatric Psychiatry, and he will be giving a poster presentation about his work at the 2013 annual conference. Max feels that Alzheimer's research is very important. He recently shared with us that "not only are these patients and their caregivers suffering, but the approaching Alzheimer's tsunami will bankrupt our already hurting healthcare system. My experiences with this disease have elucidated my lifelong path to tackle the disease on multiple fronts, encompassing compassionate care of those afflicted, support for weary caregivers, and research to find treatments and, perhaps, a cure."

CHAPTER FIVE

R.L. WILSON
INDIO, CALIFORNIA
Brothers Amazingly and Intellectually Talented
Winter 2013, Age 19

"Make sure you're doing what you're doing for the right reasons. Make sure it's coming from your heart and that you're not doing it just to be cool or just to be noticed by your peers. Do it because you're passionate about it and simply because you know that in doing what you want to do, you're going to make a difference you can be proud of. If you're proud of it, no one can take that away from you."

Nineteen-year-old R.L. Wilson said he doesn't try to combat stereotypes. Instead, he tries to change them entirely.

That is the goal of the organization Wilson founded, *Brothers Amazingly Intellectual and Talented*, a group that goes by the acronym BAIT.

Through BAIT, Wilson and his colleagues hope to create a "new, positive stereotype" of young black men as poets, artists, and intellectuals.

Wilson said that in the past, he has been pigeonholed primarily as an athlete – a talented high school basketball player.

"Back in high school really, all that I cared about was basketball," he said. "But one year I broke my wrist and poetry was the one outlet I used to express my feelings, because I didn't really talk as much back then. I was quiet, so I used poetry as a tool to express what I wasn't saying at the time. So poetry became my passion, next to basketball. Since then, my creative, poetic side has just come out more and more."

Being a basketball player allowed R.L. a certain level of popularity in high school, even though he was fairly quiet.

"I learned in high school that once I got on the basketball court, people started to notice me," he said. "That's where I started to get popular and I had friends on the court, but also off the court," he said. "Throughout my four years of high school, that's the thing that was my constant – basketball was the thing I always fell back on."

But a serious foot injury, followed by an on-court epiphany about his parents' separation and some concern about an enlarged aorta, led R.L. away from basketball, pushing him to explore his creative side instead.

R.L. shared that he had this life-changing epiphany on his birthday, November 30th.

"We were playing against a team out of the Inland Empire (of southern California) and I got a rebound and I came down and I crossed one dude over and then I looked up in the stands and I saw my parents – well, I saw my dad and my brother, then I looked up further down the line and I saw my mom sitting by herself. You know, my parents were away from each other, and I just said to myself, 'Why am I doing this?' And I lost that focus. There was no point in playing basketball anymore. My dad, to this day, doesn't fully understand why I did that. He probably still thinks I could have made it pro, but I didn't see it for myself, so I just stopped playing. Now I train with my dad. I train athletes. I'm still close to the game, but it's not the same."

A Change of Heart

Instead of building a career around basketball, R.L. now attends Langston University in Langston, Oklahoma on a Regents Scholarship. He is heavily involved in campus life in various leadership roles, including his position within BAIT.

The five other founding members of BAIT are Glen Sanchez, Eugene DeLoach, Shaquille Anderson, Eugene Buckman Jr., Kenneth Crowley Jr., and Marcus Whitefield. Glen is from California, while Eugene D., Shaquille, and Marcus are from Oklahoma and Eugene C. and Kenneth are natives of Colorado.

The group was created to promote maturity and "the growth of intellectual wisdom through poetry and the spoken word." BAIT strives to advance an interest in poetry, while also "displaying a message of advancement" and promoting "the rebirth of the African American male." The group performs poetry at schools, churches, universities, and other venues. The group's ultimate goal is to encourage other young people to explore their own poetic talents and to help them advance their educations.

Finding Motivation

R.L. said he is particularly motivated by his younger brother, Ozell Wilson, who is three years his junior: "I saw how my younger brother was going to turn out, so I put it upon myself to become a better role model, so Ozell would know the right way to do things and how to lead himself to overcome obstacles. I give him a lot of credit for my drive and motivation. I would not be who I am today if he was not in my life."

He also readily credits his parents for his motivation and success: "My parents instilled in me the values of how to be an astute African American male in today's society," he said. "My mom – I can still remember when she was teaching me my ABCs and everything; she would make me repeat the phrase 'I am somebody' over and over again until I said it with some conviction. But my dad showed me how to be a man and how to handle myself in tough situations I might face. He has always said to me that image is everything, so I made sure that I acted and looked presentable at all times because you never know who is watching."

R.L. revealed that he also is motivated by his name, which he shares with his grandfather, who was known as a leader in his community.

"Ever since I was little, people reminded me of who I was named after and told me not to bring shame to the name. So it just motivated me to be who I am. Before I left for college, I promised my grandma that I would not tarnish my grandfather's name and that I would do my best to measure up to the man that he was."

Overcoming Challenges

R.L. said the biggest challenge involved in leading BAIT has been getting to a point where he trusts others to do their part to make events successful.

"I still have this feeling sometimes like they are not going to show up," he said of other youth volunteers with BAIT. "They always *do* show up, but I'm just waiting for that feeling of uncertainty to dissolve so I can – so we can all be comfortable with one another. That's the biggest thing."

He said that building BAIT's name recognition is another large challenge.

"I want to be able to expand. And that's where Facebook and Twitter and YouTube come in. That's big. And that's what we are working on."

On his Age and Generation

R.L. said he thinks being young is usually an advantage in his work.

"People always think I'm older and then when they find out I'm doing all these things and I'm only nineteen – well, eighteen at the time I started – they're very surprised. I'm sort of becoming a role model at my university because I'm not waiting for things to be given to me. I'm just doing it. I really believe that age shouldn't be a factor in whether you achieve something or not. It should motivate you to do it while you're young because then it's that much greater of an accomplishment."

Overall, R.L. does not seem to look too optimistically on his generation, lamenting that many of his peers value quick fame over hard work and earning a good reputation.

He believes that many of the negative media portrayals of his generation are true.

"This generation has been based around material things and how you look and not necessarily what you're saying and how you appeal to other people," he said. "And so getting involved in this type of work isn't attractive to a lot of young people because you're not seen as much. You don't do it to be recognized, you do it because it's the right thing to do. You do it because it's a part of your passion and what you're trying to accomplish. It's not – it can become a very big thing to the world, but it takes time and that's what, you know, is not very attractive to my generation."

He said that his generation is often most motivated by fame – fleeting or otherwise.

"People get caught up with whatever's on TV. The quickest way to become a star is through YouTube, whether you're dancing or you're singing, or through athletics. So that's basically what my generation has built itself up on – the quickest way to get the stardom and fame."

R.L. has committed himself to being one of the young leaders who helps change his generation's obsession with such fleeting, fly-by-night fame.

Spreading the Word through Social Media

R.L. said that he finds it difficult to imagine doing his work without social networking.

"Word of mouth isn't the way," he said. "Hearsay is not the way you're going to be heard. You really have to be willing to put yourself on YouTube, and whether or not you get that many views, at least you are getting your message out there about your organization and your cause. You have to be willing to go to Facebook and message a lot of people and hopefully strike an interest in them. Without social media, it would be hard to communicate with others. A lot of opportunities have arisen from Facebook – social media has helped us out a lot."

Celebrating Successes

R.L. shared that graduating from high school and getting a scholarship to Langston University have been two of his biggest accomplishments.

He said he also cares deeply about what members of his family, including his parents and his siblings, think of him.

"My little brother said to me the other day that he thought I was stupid – an idiot, actually – for quitting basketball because he felt that, you know, I'm good at it, so why would I quit. And for the longest time he said he didn't look up to me the same as he used to since I quit, because he didn't know what I was going to do. But now he sees that what I'm doing now is bigger than basketball and I think it's making him reevaluate why he wants to do sports and if he even wants to play them because he sees, from my example, that sports are not everything. You can't live between the lines and boundaries of what people expect you to do. He sees that you can do what you want to do – what's in your heart. So, I think that's one of my biggest accomplishments, just motivating him to expand his horizons."

On his Future

R.L. hopes to graduate from college early and to continue his work with BAIT, including officially establishing it as a non-profit organization later this spring. He also wants to manage other people's careers, including that of a childhood friend who wants to be a producer and of another who seems to be NBA bound.

"I'm not really trying to stick to one career. I want multiple careers, hopefully. We'll see what happens."

The teen said he views college as the launching pad for the rest of his life.

"It's where it all begins," he stated. "At the beginning of my senior year in high school, my dad told me that my name is my company, so I need to build my company in the way that I want it to be seen. So college is where I've made most of my connections. And really, the time spent at college should help build the foundation of what you want to do throughout your life. You really need to take all the opportunities presented to you, even if these opportunities are not things that you would normally do – you never know what doors may open."

Learning from his Mistakes

R.L. shared that one of his biggest mistakes has been not doing a better job of keeping up with people from his high school days. He attended a total of six different high schools, and sometimes burned bridges when he changed schools.

"I didn't let anyone know I was transferring. I just left. And I think – well, I know through hearing from the people I do talk to – a lot of people did not like me too much after I left because I was just there one day and then gone the next. If I had kept in contact with most of them, then this process of what I'm trying to build now would be much easier because they would support me in a way. Now I have to work that much harder to find friends who know me and will support me in the same way."

Handling Criticism

Being an athlete has taught him how to take criticism. "A lot of people are going to criticize you because either they don't like that you are as good as you are or they are trying to help you to get better," he said.

He said he had a coach that was particularly critical.

"He criticized me a lot. It was overbearing at times, but I knew why he was doing it. He saw the potential in me, and so I took that and used it to help myself. It was constructive criticism, even though I didn't realize it at the time. I thought he was just trying to degrade me in a way. But now I see that it's not a bad thing to be criticized because if people are criticizing you, then it means you have potential to be better than what you are at that point. So now I embrace it."

Drawing on Strengths

The teen also embraces his background and believes the fact that he attended six different high schools has pushed him to learn how to appeal to different types of people, often from the role of an outsider.

"I know how to talk to people and how to relate to people," he said. "I'm also very persistent, very determined. And also, I'm humble. I don't think people feel threatened to come up and talk to me about anything. But my weakness is that sometimes I'm afraid to step out and lead. Like starting BAIT – I'm not trying to be a visible leader, in a way. I don't mind being the leader behind the scenes in order to let others be the ones seen in front of crowds. And I think that's a weakness sometimes because if they don't know who it's coming from, how will they know how to like and relate to it?"

A Message to Adults

He said he thinks today's adults need to recognize that times are changing.

"It's not the same way it was back in the day," he said. "When our parents and teachers were kids, they knew that things were changing when their parents were scolding them. So if they want to understand where we're coming from now, it would be a whole lot easier if they could all realize that times are changing. They weren't really always understood by adults when they were young, and now that they are the adults, they don't understand, either. Things repeat."

Still, he said he has empathy for adults, and thinks they often are trying to do what's best.

"At times it's about being seen as an adult and not just another friend," he said. "I see where both sides are coming from."

He said he thinks more adults could build relationships with young people if they were willing to "break out of their shells."

"It's about just trying to do some of the stuff we're doing now with Facebook and Twitter and just trying to gel with today's generation," he explained.

Defining Success

R.L. defines individual success as "just being happy, really."

He said that if you can achieve happiness, you have gotten the most possible out of life.

"If you're happy with what you're doing and where you're going in life, that is success. Everybody's success is different. Some people might not want to be the famous TV star and be seen and might not want to be the owner of a corporation. They might just want to grow up and get a job and have a family. Everybody's success is different, so I base it off whether that person is happy or not. Because if you're happy, whatever you're doing at that time is your success."

Within his organization, R.L. said he defines success as reaching as many people as he can, and also as building deep relationships with people. And he is already thinking about the importance of passing his work off to the next generation.

"We want to have real fans – people who understand why we're doing what we do and where we're coming from – people that will just stick with us wherever and whatever we do. I just really want to be this catalyst for the younger generation coming up. Hopefully they will want to do something positive like what we have started and just try to keep it going."

Still, he admitted there are times when it is tempting to quit.

"It's hard to do something with no clear reward in the beginning," he said. "With no one patting you on the back, letting you know that you're doing great and you're doing it for the right reasons. This type of work is based upon self-motivation and what you want to give back to your community, your state, and the world. What has motivated me to keep on going is the knowledge that if I don't do it, someone else will. And if they do it and it becomes something that you thought it would be, then it's theirs and not yours. So you might as well get up and do it now before someone else does, because somebody will come up with the same idea as you, but they might not do it in the way you would have if you had taken the initiative."

He said his biggest piece of advice for young people is to regularly check their motivation.

"I would say make sure you're doing what you're doing for the right reasons," he said. "Make sure that it's coming from your heart and that you're not doing it just to be cool or just to be noticed by your peers. Do it because you're passionate about it and simply because you know that in doing what you want to do, you're going to make a difference you can be proud of. If you're proud of it, no one can take that away from you. The joy that you get from doing what you enjoy, that's something that's yours and you're in control of that, so just do it because you enjoy it and you like doing it. That's where it should come from - your heart - and you can't go wrong."

R.L. shared a lot with us during our meetings, often circling back to stories of high school and how hard it was to attend six different schools.

After the main interview concluded, he smiled, paused and said, "That was so cool – just being able to talk about my life and my experiences. I feel important, like I actually have something to share that people are going to want to listen to."

Indeed, R.L. Indeed.

Update

We first met R.L. early in 2012, but did not actually sit down with him for this interview until January of 2013. In addition to being a full-time college student and founder and leader of BAIT, he is also involved in university life in a number of other ways. In the capacity of a Student Ambassador, he works as a mentor and consular for all incoming freshmen. His work involves everything from tutoring new students in their academic classes to helping them get acclimated to college life. The most important thing R.L. does in this role, he shared, is "just being a good example to the freshmen in any way that I can." He is part of the Academic Committee, where he serves as a juror dealing with students who violate collegiate rules. He also is the student representative on the Budget Planning Committee with university administrators, serving as the voice of the students when the committee votes on issues that affect the school, ranging from "whether to cut certain athletic programs or fund future student scholarships." Additionally, he is employed in the Office of the Vice President for Student Affairs and not only works directly with the VP, but also helps students to determine who they should talk to when they are faced with various challenges and issues. He is also working on establishing BAIT as an official non-profit organization and hopes to obtain this designation by late spring.

CHAPTER SIX

SHAYLEE HATCH
NAMPA, IDAHO
The Temporary Home Foundation
Late Fall 2011, Age 18

"Once you help someone, they're impacted and get that good spirit, too. And they just want to go out and help others and it's just so cool to see that big chain reaction starting."

"Are you really sure about this?"

This was the question that Shaylee asked us repeatedly during our first interview. Even though her non-profit, *The Temporary Home Foundation*, was well underway and she was recognized as a leader among her peers and in her community, Shaylee did not seem to view herself the same way others did.

We found her dubious reaction to our interest compelling – and also think it is one of the reasons her story is so important. She views herself, above all, as a typical teenager – just a young person trying to use her talents and resources to help the people around her in any way she can.

Shaylee's Work

When Shaylee was a sophomore in high school, she began fundraising for a number of causes in her community. This initial fundraising work ignited a spark in her, pushing her to do more to aid people around her.

One of her first projects was helping with *Wheels for Grant*, a benefit for a seven-year-old boy in her community who had cerebral palsy and needed an electric wheelchair in order to get around with more ease and comfort.

"He was the oldest of four children," Shaylee explained. "He was always having to be pushed in his wheelchair by his mom, but his mom had three other younger kids to take care of and it was just really hard on them."

The family also had endured a number of financial struggles, like countless other families during the recent economic meltdown. There was no money in the budget for an electric wheelchair – or for much else in the way of "extras."

Shaylee said as soon as she heard about the family's situation, she knew she had to help.

"We got together with them and we just stood outside of a few local grocery stores and called the radio stations," she said. "They helped advertise it and, since Grant loves football, I got some of my friends from the high school football team to help out. The football coaches even allowed us to send donation buckets around at a home game and honored Grant as a special guest at that game. After a lot of hard work from his parents, community members, and fundraisers, we ended up raising $10,000 all together. With the money we raised, Grant got his special electric wheelchair with the attachment part to it that he can use to help himself stand up by himself without outside assistance."

With the new wheelchair, Grant was able to go to the restroom by himself, get a drink from the water fountain, and do work at the whiteboard at school without having to ask anyone for help, she said.

Gaining Momentum

Her experience with Grant and his family allowed Shaylee to see how just a little bit of effort and organization could go a long way toward making a sizable difference in the lives of people in need.

That same school year, Shaylee lost a friend to cancer.

The friend was receiving treatment at the St. Luke's Mountain States Tumor Institute (MSTI), the only children's treatment center in Boise, Idaho. At about the same time, Shaylee and her classmates were given a group assignment in school – to do something to better their community.

"I talked to my group," Shaylee explained, "and I told them 'You know, a lot of people don't really think about the kids at the cancer center. It's not that they're forgotten or anything, but in our everyday lives we are so busy and we don't always think about those who are less fortunate than we are. We have our health.'"

So Shaylee and her classmates got together and told the community about what they were doing. They stood outside of grocery stores, passed out fliers, and managed to raise a few thousand dollars through their efforts. With this money, they were able to purchase five shopping carts of new toys and books to deliver to the cancer center. Shaylee said that "it was just overwhelming to see how – in just a few short days of raising money – we were able to positively affect so many lives. The little kids at the hospital were just so *happy*. And that's what made me really want to start a non-profit and start helping people."

Shaylee said one of the things that remained with her from these early philanthropic efforts was the idea that even a little effort could do so much to bring about change.

"We did the project to raise money for the kids with cancer and got them things and I was just overwhelmed at how amazing it was," she said. "And we honestly spent two or three days at the most getting organized and fundraising. It was just crazy to me how giving the community was and just to be able to see that I actually made an impact in someone's life totally changed my whole perspective and made me want to help people further."

The Temporary Home

At the time of our first interview, Shaylee was in the beginning stages of developing her non-profit organization, *The Temporary Home Foundation.*

The goal of the foundation is to provide temporary housing to people in emergency situations.

She got the idea in part through her work in Joplin, Missouri, where she volunteered in the aftermath of devastating tornadoes.

"Just seeing all the people who lost their houses and their families – it was chaotic there even months after the tornado happened and that totally affected me and so one part of *The Temporary Home Foundation* will focus on helping people get houses and helping them get their lives back after natural disasters," she explained.

She also wants to help provide housing to people who might be homeless for other reasons. She has a particular interest in the young people who are exiting foster care with nowhere to go and no one to help them out.

"I've had a few friends who were in the foster care system and when they turn eighteen the state gives them money, but they don't always have a set path or a place to go," she reflected. "I want to help foster kids have a good temporary home and to help them figure out where they're going to go next. I realized there was this big need, because a lot of them end up getting pregnant or going to jail. And a lot of them don't feel like they have a promising future, but that's only because they really don't have anyone there to help. I want to help with that as well – just to help show them people care and even though they have been in foster care, they still deserve the same opportunities as anyone else. I respect them so much because I can't even imagine not having a family or friends – people who are always there for you. I think it would be really hard."

She also serves on the Youth Advisory Board of *Idaho Drug Free Youth*. In that role, she has helped to select the theme for an annual youth summit attended by students from across the state. She also has had the opportunity to speak at different conferences and to raise money for the organization.

She said the organization's message is simple: "To empower youth to lead happy and healthy lives. *Idaho Drug Free Youth* provides youth in our state the opportunity to empower themselves as well as their peers and other community members by giving them leadership roles in their communities and schools. And it's fun!"

Shaylee went on to share that *Idaho Drug Free Youth* (IDFY) helps educate youth and parents about the harmful effects of underage drinking and drug use, and also provides positive peer and adult influences throughout communities in the state of Idaho.

Shaylee said that IDFY teaches young people that, "If you get offered drugs, you can say, 'No I can't' – first of all because you don't want to do drugs, but also because you don't have to be scared of what people think of you because you can just say no."

She said the organization also gives students advice on how to lower the social stakes when saying no to drugs. For example, athletes might resist drug use because they are concerned about drug testing, or students might say they are worried their parents know the signs of drug abuse and are watching.

Finding Motivation

Shaylee said that when she sees people in need she is not overwhelmed or discouraged – instead, she uses the realities of life to motivate her to do more.

"Sometimes we might go caroling at the foster care group homes or we go to the elderly homes and see people who just need help," she said. "That totally motivates me and makes me want to go out there and try to help as many people as I can. Then, it's awesome to just see the chain reaction it starts. Once you help someone they're impacted and get that good spirit, too, and they just want to go out and help others and it's just so cool to see that big chain reaction starting."

She said her family's focus on helping others also has been a strong inspiration and motivation: "My parents taught me early on in life that helping people was very important. I'm so lucky for that!" Her great grandmother, Alma Zuna, was a particularly powerful role model.

"She was probably the most giving person I've ever met and she just always said what was on her mind. We had a talk one day, and she was like, you know, make sure when you grow up you know there's always people less fortunate than you. And not many people think of them. They just tend to think of themselves, so *you* need to be the one to go help out. Ever since I can remember, I have just tried to live by my great grandmother's words. She's probably been my main motivation."

Shaylee acknowledged that asking people for support is not always easy – particularly during times when the economy has faltered and people have been more cautious with their money.

"It's kind of hard to get as much money as you need to because you want to help in just so many ways," she said. "But in order to help people you need funds and you need people to jump on board to help out and that's a challenge as well."

The Impact of Youth

Shaylee talked openly about how she saw her age as both an advantage and disadvantage to the work she does.

On one hand, she said it is comforting and exciting to know she likely has a lot of time left in her lifetime to help others.

"I look at it and I have so many more years left to help others," she said. "I'm just starting out and I'm looking into my future and there're just so many awesome things I'm going to be able to do and so many more people I'm going to be able to help and so in a way, the possibilities are endless. For me, it's so exciting to think about how I'm only eighteen, because I have so many more years to do so many awesome things."

But not everyone sees her youth as an advantage, and sometimes that reality is tough to accept, she revealed.

"I'd have to say that maybe the number one challenge has been having people take me seriously. I don't know. I just turned eighteen and not that I was super young or anything but sometimes people look at me and are like, 'Are you serious? Why are you doing these things?' It's like sometimes they expect me not to follow through with what I say and that's been kind of hard."

Shaylee then went on to challenge the stereotype her generation has often been saddled with about being apathetic.

She said that although she thinks this stereotype is "why so many people are so surprised and don't take me seriously," she also sees challenging the label as exciting – even exhilarating.

She elaborated by saying, "It's been so cool because with a few of the fundraisers we've done at my high school, like *Change for Haiti* for example, so many kids have been willing to help out who are my age, from freshmen to seniors. I had tons of people willing to help and everyone's like, 'What do you need and how can I help you?' and that's been amazing to see because there is kind of a bad view of young people and it's just awesome to see young people getting involved. I just wish more adults could see how some of the young people just don't know how to get started, but once something is started they're just right on board and helping out."

She said that sometimes she thinks her generation is misunderstood because of its use of and interest in technology.

"Honestly, when you just kind of listen to what everyone says about our generation – that we're lazy or that we don't know how to work hard or that social networking and texting are all we do – that's just so negative!" she said.

Shaylee stated that generational stereotypes make her uncomfortable – and are generally unfair.

"I think what people just need to know is that there's good and bad in every situation and not every young person is the same. There are some troubled ones and that's totally fine. Maybe they'll grow out of it or maybe that's just who they are," she said. "And then there are some outstanding young people. And I think people need to not just judge us on only one specific idea or thing. I don't know, you can't just categorize people. We're all so different and we all have different standards, morals and goals – we all come from different backgrounds. You can't really categorize our generation. And what you hear a lot about our generation is mostly negative things. It's really sad because I know some amazing young people, and I'm sure everyone does. If we could just focus more on that and just uplift others instead of just tearing them down, that would help."

She said the economic woes of the last few years have challenged her generation, and even discouraged some young people from pushing themselves harder.

"People are stressed out about the economy and school and no one can afford anything," she said.

Still, despite all those financial concerns, Shaylee believes that today's generation also is excited and optimistic about its future and retains the sense that anything can still happen.

"I think what's exciting to us – at least I know my classmates and I discuss this – is that we know we have a future ahead of us and we're about to start our future and that's exciting because we can all go in whatever direction we want to go," she said. "We're lucky to live in the United States where we have tons of different options. You can go to college if you want to, you can go into any field and that's definitely something that excites the youth now because we just have tons of opportunities. Some of them want to play pro sports or be singers or doctors or lawyers. And something I know now is when people say you can be or do whatever you want, it's not a fairytale line – it can be achieved through hard work. Probably just the main excitement is knowing that if you follow what you want to do and make it happen, it will actually happen."

Connecting with Adults

Shaylee said she doesn't think that there is a magical formula for adults interested in connecting with her generation.

But she said that making those connections is not as difficult as many adults seem to think.

"It's really simple," she said. "I've had a few teachers these past few years at Skyview High School who have made me realize that the sky is the limit. They helped me realize this simply by pointing out that they knew I loved helping people and that I was smart enough to go to college and to never question the idea that if you work hard, you'll reach your goals. Joie Gariaga, my choir teacher, helped me develop my fundraising and leadership skills; Kelli Hannum, my English teacher, helped me realize that through hard work I could succeed academically; Hailey Croft, my communications teacher, taught me not to give up on my dreams and go for it; and my basketball coach, Cindy Pasta, showed me what hard work can do and how many people it can affect in a positive way. These adults and many more believed in me when I was unsure of myself and taught me things I needed to learn and know to be able to start my future. Having them reach out to me has made a lifetime impact; they went above and beyond their teaching jobs to help me and I will be forever grateful."

"You know, it's so simple but we just need to be talked to. Not talked down to or nagged all the time, but just talked to. So if adults sit down and talk to us it just helps so much. Sometimes we put our heads down when our parents come in and try to talk to us. But honestly deep down most kids want their parents' time and they just want their time to be talked to. Make sure you ask your kids what they want in their future and support them in their dreams, no matter how unrealistic those dreams might seem to you. And know we'll probably change our minds a hundred times in the process of figuring out what we need and want. But keep talking to us! It helps so much. It's amazing – it's so simple, but it goes so far."

The Power of Social Media

Shaylee acknowledged that without social media, she would face many more challenges in her work.

"Without social networking, the work I do would be so hard," she said. "Social media is a great way to tell people when a fundraiser is going on or to get people to help because it's hard to spread the word through just speaking to people. I mean, that's kind of easy, except you're not always around people, so through social networking you can reach more people. That's one key part for setting things up because the radio stations here in Boise have helped me so much. When I have fundraisers they just get on air, even if it's just for a minute of their time, they just get on and tell people where the fundraiser's going to be, what time, and if they want to help out where to go, and that's just been a huge help. And without that, spreading the word about the projects I'm working on would be so hard."

"I know a lot of adults look at social networking as a downfall or something that a lot of kids are addicted to, and I can see that side as well. There's definitely both upsides and downfalls with using social media, but it is being used for good things too, so try to be open-minded."

Choosing a Different Path

Shaylee said that college is a big priority for her – even while her non-profit work has taken off.

"There are just so many goals I want to accomplish in my life and so many people I want to just go out and help, but I can't just jump into it. I need to be patient."

She hopes to major in social work and minor in business – partly so she can learn more about the nuts and bolts of running a non-profit, and also to research how to most effectively help people.

"I think having that structure is definitely going to help me be way more successful in my non-profit and I think education in and of itself is very important because you just learn and grow while you're in college and I'm excited for the experience."

Making Mistakes

Shaylee said some of her biggest mistakes were made at home growing up – like when she argued with her parents over chores and other responsibilities.

"I have fought with them over dumb things like chores – things that would have taken me five minutes to complete. I wish I could go back and just redo that."

She also has some minor academic regrets.

"My freshman year I kind of didn't take school as seriously as I should have and the same thing with my sophomore year. I mean I went to classes and I did most of – well, I did some of the homework. I'm not going to lie, I didn't always do it. It wasn't until my junior and senior year that I planned on going to college. I was actually planning on going to hair school because I love hair and makeup and that's just fun and then I sat down and – well, I never really had a plan – and planning is definitely an important part for your future because you kind of have to have one. Some people can just roll with it and that's great, but I'm a planner and

I have to have a plan, so I wish I would have taken school more seriously when I was younger and taken advantage of some more opportunities, I guess."

She also wishes she had explored more extracurricular opportunities in the early years of high school.

"In high school I finally got involved in things my junior year. I was in *Rachel's Challenge*, I was in *Idaho Drug Free Youth*, I was in all of the school choirs, I played basketball, and I was in leadership. And that was all really fun, but I wish I had done it sooner, and I wish kids all over would get involved because it makes such a big difference. You meet so many people and you don't really think about how being involved in things like that can help you in your future – I didn't really know all I was capable of until I started to really get out there and so I wish I would have done that a little sooner."

She said that the change came for her when she realized she was waiting for her life to start – waiting to make the right choices and to seize all the opportunities around her.

"I was just sitting there, I just got home one day and I was like, you know, just thinking about some of the people I knew at my school and I was like, 'Oh they're just so cool and I wish that I could make everything look that easy or I wish that I could have what they have.' And I was sitting there thinking, 'I'm kind of sick of just thinking about all the things I want to do one day' and so I got up and did it."

"And it wasn't even hard. I thought it was going to be so hard and at times there were a few little challenges and bumps, and that's part of it, but I'm looking back on it now and I'm just so happy I decided to just get out there and do it because I thought about doing it and I wanted to do it, but it took me just getting out there and actually doing it to realize all I was capable of."

She said that she didn't have much tolerance for criticism when she started her work. But slowly, she has come to recognize that positive criticism can bring improvement.

"You know, I used to not like criticism at all. Oh man, I just wasn't really good at handling it. I just let it hurt my feelings. And then I realized, you know what, criticism makes me a better person because I know what I need to fix and I know what I need to work on and I just was looking at it through a different perspective. Criticism can be good or bad, but either way it's going to strengthen me and if it's bad criticism maybe it's something I need to fix and if it's good, maybe it's something I need to do more of and so now I'm trying to handle it in a good way."

She said she has learned how to better handle criticism at home, too.

"When I was younger and my mom was like, 'You didn't do this right, so come re-do it,' it was never to put me down; it was to teach me to not only do things, but to do them right. And then I kind of grew up and now I appreciate getting criticism – sometimes it's hard to take, but if you can just roll with it you can grow and learn so much and see things you need to fix and make better."

Through criticism and self-reflection, she has come to better recognize her own strengths and weaknesses as well.

She said one of her biggest strengths is her outgoing personality – something that she developed with age, as she got more practice at reaching out to others and sharing her ideas.

"I used to be all shy and quiet, but now that I'm outgoing I love meeting new people and talking to people. This helps a lot with what I'm doing in my life because if I want to go out and promote a non-profit or help tons of people I can't do that if I'm too scared to talk to them, so I think that's kind of a good strength."

She sees her weaknesses with equal clarity.

"I'm not perfect in any way or even close – when I have a lot going on sometimes I don't finish things. I know when I have too much going on I need to just slow down and focus on little things one step at a time. That's my biggest fault. I try to run into something without taking one day at a time and taking it slow."

Organizational Needs

She said her organization has a number of big needs.

"I want to help as many people as I can," she said. "And it's my dream to have a huge non-profit. Obviously funding is a huge part of it, but as a college student I'm a little worried because it will take a few years to get a huge organization because I still need to put myself through school. So funding is a huge one. And perseverance. I know I'm going to reach my goal, but there's probably going to be a few times when I'm like, 'This is really, really hard.' I know it's going to be hard and sometimes I might just want to stop, but I'm just never going to. And I know it will all be worth it in the end. I'm excited to see the outcome, it will just take me a few years to set it all up."

She defined personal success as setting goals and reaching them.

"Success is just doing what you say you're going to do and doing it 100 percent and not stopping."

And for her organization, being seen as a source of help to many is a major goal.

"If people are victims of a natural disaster in the world and lose their homes and everything they had, I want them to know exactly who to call to come help. I just want to be available for people to call to go help them. I cannot wait to go out and just help as many people as I can and to me that will be success."

Despite her broad vision, Shaylee also has days when she is tempted to just sit back and relax, choosing entertainment over work.

"As much fun as hanging out with friends is and just hanging out on the couch, those are awesome days. But I just think about opportunities I've had in my life and the people I've been able to help so far and it amazes me and motivates me even more because I just want to go out there and help even more people and go to different places in the world and help. I'm just motivated when I think about all the possibilities out there and so many different ways to help people. So I know it's going to be a super long road ahead of me, but I'm not going to stop because the possibilities are endless. As cheesy as that sounds, it's so true."

Of all her achievements, Shaylee said she is most proud of her success in helping raise money for Grant's family to purchase a wheelchair and of having the opportunity to be a big part of *Idaho Drug Free Youth.*

"It didn't just affect one person, Grant. It was his whole family. And it was just amazing to see how happy he was with his wheelchair and he can't really use his hands very well – he only has one hand that works well – so to be able to see him be independent just totally affected me and I didn't think I'd ever be able to help somebody like that. So that was probably my biggest achievement."

She said that she sees marriage and family in her future. She also would love to have some big-name celebrities, including Carrie Underwood, sing at some of her benefit events for *The Temporary Home Foundation.*

She has already made progress toward this goal, since she talked to Underwood on the phone through a radio station that was advertising Shaylee's fundraising efforts.

"She has a song, *Temporary Home*, that just really affected me and one day I just want her to perform at one of my organization's fundraisers. I love Carrie Underwood's songs and the messages in them. Her song *Change* is one I listen to if I am ever feeling discouraged. The chorus says, 'Don't listen to them when they say you're just a fool to believe you can change the world.' I just love that! So those are some of my big dreams. She's such a big role model of mine. She helps so many people and she went to college and had a chance and took it – she followed her dreams and with hard work and talent she won *American Idol* and now look at her! She is living her dreams. She made it happen and that's so awesome and inspiring to me!"

The teen also hopes for her organization to ultimately have an international focus.

"I want to travel the world and help people and go to Haiti and Africa and help people in my own community as well, you know, but I want to broaden my journey a little bit and get out there and see the world as well. "

Update

We interviewed Shaylee for this book in the fall of 2011. We've kept up with her since then, as she's graduated high school, moved away to college, and then moved back to her hometown.

In February of this year she sent us the following update: "I am now nineteen years old. I attended BYU-Idaho in Rexburg, Idaho for two semesters and lived there for almost a year – working and going to school – when I decided I was going to accomplish one of my dreams! I moved back to Nampa, Idaho and started hair school at the *Velvet Touch Academy of Cosmetology* in September 2012. I am still attending and will graduate from there in September 2013. I am also taking college classes online, so I'm moving forward in school as well and pursuing my bachelor's degree. I've always been interested in doing hair and I feel it fits perfectly with my goals of running my non-profit, *The Temporary Home Foundation*. My goal is to have my own in-home hair salon established within the next five years so that I can take care of my financial needs, while also having the time and flexibility to run my non-profit organization and help other people. I am still in the beginning process of my non-profit, but I wouldn't have it any other way! I look forward to the day when I will be able to make that dream come true and help as many people as I can. I am so blessed to be where I am in my life right now!"

"It has been such a huge honor and experience to be able to have this opportunity to share my story and be in the same book as these other young people who are doing such great things! It's incredible and to be a part of this book is by far the biggest blessing. I just want to thank my parents, Jack and Holly Hatch, and my siblings. I want to thank my grandparents, Donna and David Porter and Jean and Max Hatch, as well as all of my extended family, aunts, uncles, and cousins. I want to thank my *Young Women Leaders* because without their great example I'm not sure if I would be where I am today. I want to thank Brannan and Brittany Hoover for being my family and helping and believing in me every step of the way up at college, all of my teachers and friends from Skyview High School, my "Velvet Touch family," *Idaho Drug Free Youth* non-profit organization and all of those involved with this incredible organization. I also want to thank my community – I'm blessed to live in Nampa, Idaho with such great people! Dr. Marina V. Gillmore, Keith L. Brown and Dr. Monique Henderson, thank you will never be enough for giving me the opportunity to share my story and to be able to be a part of a project like this. It has been so amazing and by far the most humbling and exciting thing I have experienced. Thanks for all of your hard work, dedication and time – it is people like you who help make our dreams a reality!"

The most recent update we received from Shaylee was that she had talked to Grant's mom, and "found out that the wheelchair I helped get him is being used as an important part of his therapy!" The excitement in her voice was palpable: "His mom said that in order to slow the deterioration of his muscles, his therapy plan involves standing at least ten hours a week. And he can do that with his wheelchair! I had no idea, back when I helped raise money for the wheelchair, what an important part of his life it would really become! It's just the greatest feeling to know I've helped improve his life."

CONCLUSION

We know the voices of the six young people highlighted in this book are powerful because there is an authenticity to them that is contagious. As different as their lives and their organizations are, they share a common passion for doing their part to make the world a better place.

And at the end of the day, this isn't a passion we take lightly. We believe it's a zeal that needs to be celebrated without being trivialized and supported without being exploited.

Joe, Jordan, Max, MaryPat, R.L., and Shaylee are visionaries, but they are also in need of the guidance and support of the adults in their lives. Because, for all their eloquence, intelligence, and confidence, they are also young. And they wanted to make sure that – throughout the times we spent with them – we didn't forget that.

For any young people who are inspired by the stories you've read here, we encourage you to learn from their experiences and act upon whatever dream you have of making the world a better place. The message is not that if you are inspired by MaryPat, for example, you need to be *exactly* like MaryPat, but rather that you take whatever you may have found inspiring in her story, her voice, or her purpose, and use that inspiration to spark a change in your own life that, in turn, is bound to impact those around you in ways both small and profound.

Here are a few ways to get started:

- Connect with people who share your vision. Develop a network that includes both other young people and adults who are involved in and genuinely enthused about the work you want to pursue. For example, if you are interested in social advocacy work and speaking, it would be a good idea to not only connect with young people like MaryPat and Jordan, but also some adults who are involved in this kind of work professionally. We think you will find that the young people will support you and inspire you, while the adults will be able to provide you with a worldview that comes from experience. Likewise, often adults will have access to organizations, people, and resources that might not otherwise be available to you.

- Read, read, and read some more. Research your area of interest and develop a sound understanding of the context in which you'll be working. For example, if you have a love for music and want to promote music therapy or music programs for low-income students, research all facets of music and how those in the music industry use their craft not only to better themselves, but to better the lives of others as well. Whatever your passion, make certain it is in an area that will help others have a better quality of life. And above all, do no harm.

- Develop a plan of action, but don't be afraid to get involved before you know exactly where you are going. If you know your *why*, you can often figure out your *what* and *how* along the way. For example, when we asked Jordan what advice she would give to a middle school student wanting to get involved in social justice work, she looked us dead in the eye and said, "Do it. Don't think about it. Just do it. Just start right now. What do you want to do? What do you want to accomplish and why? And do it. No limits." Shaylee echoed Jordan's sentiment when she said, "Think about what area you want to go into – because there's so many ways to help people – and just get up and go do it. That's what I did. I honestly just winged it for years. It's been great. I honestly didn't know what I was doing half of the time, but it came together and I'm on the right track with what I'm doing. I'd honestly say just discipline yourself and go and do it. Don't just sit there and say, 'Oh I'll do it later, next week, or tomorrow.' Because when tomorrow comes, half of the people who said, 'Oh, I'll do it tomorrow or I'll do it later' don't ever do anything. So I'd say just get out there and do it and get people involved because once you get people involved, it just starts a chain reaction where everyone starts to jump on board."

- We hope you hear Jordan and Shaylee's voices in your head the next time you are questioning whether you have the confidence you need to move forward into your purpose. Remember your *why* that is burning on the inside of you – that thing that pushes you to do great work to make the world a better place in which to live. The *how* and the *what* then become the steps you take to focus your passion into a clear purpose. The *why* will drive you to keep going even during the times when the *how* and the *what* may seem unclear.

- Be sure to listen to your own passions. It is easy to get caught up in the interests of others, instead of doing what speaks to you most. For example, maybe you are surrounded by people who are most passionate about providing food and shelter to people who need it. But maybe that is not your calling. Maybe what excites you most is helping to meet the needs of abused and neglected animals. Don't be afraid to do what interests you – even if the people around you do not think it is as important as you do. Or, as R.L. so eloquently stated, "You can't live between the lines and boundaries of what people expect you to do." Whatever your passion, there are people out there who will support what you are doing and who find it as important as you do.

- Don't allow yourself to be overwhelmed. There are many needs in the world. And the number of needs – and awareness about those needs – seems to grow exponentially each day. You will not be able to help everyone, but you can help someone. So do what you can, and be thankful for any opportunity to give.

- Don't be afraid to mess up and make mistakes. One of the benefits of being young is that people tend to be quite understanding when young people make honest mistakes while trying to do good work. Always do your best, but

remember that no one should expect you to be perfect –
including yourself.

And if you are a parent, teacher, or youth leader wondering how
to best support the young people in your life as they develop
passion and purpose for change, we encourage you to build your
own support network. Give your young people both the space they
need to creatively grow and the guidance they need to navigate
a complex world. One of the most important lessons we learned
from the time we spent with these incredible young people is that
the biggest gift we as adults can give them is to show them that we
not only care, but that we believe their vision is possible. Beyond
that, here are some specific ways you can support the young
people in your life:

- Honor their ideas, however ambitious or far-fetched they
  may seem to you. Remember that one of the beautiful things
  about adolescence is the ability to dream unencumbered by
  the often-harsh realities of the world in which we all live. So
  let them dream big. Challenge them to think through their
  ideas, but don't discourage their enthusiasm. They will have
  enough people in the world telling them that what they want
  to do is impossible – be that alternate voice, cheerleader, and
  sounding board that encourages them to say, "Not impossible –
  I'm possible."

- Share with them your experiences of both success and failure
  when trying new things, however small they may seem to
  you. Young people want to know what is behind your success,
  but they also want to know what you've learned from the
  mistakes you've made along the way. Therefore, don't be

afraid to be transparent with our youth. Once you do so, they will – in turn – share with you in ways you may never have thought possible.

- Remember that their passions might not be yours. Maybe you made a name for yourself in your community by starting a food pantry. Or maybe the plight of children who have been in foster care really touches your heart, and you want to see something done. You can certainly share those concerns and passions with young people. But ultimately, those are your passions, and theirs may be quite different. Give them the support and the freedom needed to find their own causes. And then support them, while also continuing to advance your own causes in new and dynamic ways.

- See their strengths. Some parents still see their teens as the impulsive toddlers or grade school children they once were, instead of who they are now. The young people in your life are surely growing, maturing, and changing. Be sure to see them for who they are now, instead of locking them in and still seeing weaknesses that may have existed years ago but have since resolved.

- Don't discount technology. Maybe you see social networking as a waste of time. Or maybe you are fearful of who your young person might get to know through online avenues. Certainly be cautious and supervise interactions carefully. But keep an open mind about how such technology might help your child to connect, share his or her vision, and grow his or her organization and cause. You are likely to be amazed!

- Don't stop encouraging and supporting, even if the young person in question already appears to have plenty of confidence and self-esteem. All of the young people in this book agreed that they and their peers crave the companionship of the adults in their lives. So, even when your young person does not seem to want to hear from you, be there. And offer help, support, and insights as often as you can. It's not going as unnoticed as it might seem.

- Let them fail. As parents and other youth leaders, this can be perhaps the hardest thing of all to do. But if we trust our young people, we also trust in their resiliency. Let them venture into the unknown and spread their wings – we believe you'll be pleasantly surprised by the results.

If there is one overarching idea that we hope to leave you with after you close this book, it is the notion that transforming the world is not something that can – or should – be left solely to those people who are viewed as having some sort of social, intellectual, or economic advantage. Instead, it is work that everyone, of all ages and backgrounds, can and arguably should do.

And because we believe so strongly in the young people featured here, we will leave you with a reiteration of something Jordan shared with us the last time we spoke with her:

"It's rare that students are keynoting conferences, lobbying in their local and federal government offices, and sitting at the decision table for organizations. Over the years, I've been looked at as exceptional for sitting at the table or being the youngest to not only speak at an event, but even receive an invitation to attend the event in the first place. I am great – I am. But there is nothing exceptional about me. I was given the opportunity to lead at a young age, and I took it. I was given the opportunity to amplify my voice at a young age, and I did. I am now focused on equipping young people with the tools they need to succeed as leaders."

The opportunities we are given look different for each of us. Some of us may have more economic resources to share. Some of us may be naturally hard-wired for leadership. Others among us find that writing or speaking come quite easily. And some of us may have yet to figure out where our strengths most clearly lie. But we all can and do have something important to offer. We have our humanity. And we have compassion. And we have a vested interest in making the world a better place, both today and in the future.

We hope the words, ideas, and actions of the young people featured in this book stick with you and inspire you as they have inspired us. We hope you find yourself repeating some of the stories told here to your friends, family, colleagues, and others. We hope that you share this book with someone else and that he or she, in turn, passes it along.

And we hope that as you think about these young people, you will be challenged yourself to make the most of where you are and what you have, so that you may share with those around you. And that in some way you, your community, and the world will be transformed in the process. There is much work left to be done. Each of us has a responsibility to get busy doing it.

What will you do?

GROUP DISCUSSION GUIDES

It is our intention that this book be used, in part, to spark conversation and dialogue both within groups of adults and young people, and among them. For that reason, we have provided three separate discussion guides in the pages that follow: a reader's group discussion guide for adults, a reader's group discussion guide for youth and young adults, and a reader's group discussion guide for combined youth-adult study. May you be inspired not only by the stories you've read in the pages of this book, but also by the conversations that come about as a result of these stories.

Reader's Group Discussion Guide for Adults

1. All six of the young people in this book talked extensively about the adults in their lives who have inspired, encouraged, and supported them. They mentioned parents and teachers, but also family members and leaders, both formal and informal. Who are the youth that you have the opportunity to encourage and inspire? How might you do more to encourage and inspire the young people within your sphere of influence?

2. Some of the young people we featured talked about their struggles to be heard in spite of their youth. Are you ever

guilty of minimizing the words of young people — either because of their age or because they do not communicate the same way you and the other adults in your life generally do? Have you ever stood by while others trivialized the words or ideas of young people? How might you do things differently in the future?

3. The current generation has been criticized by some for being too focused on texting and social media, instead of face-to-face communication. Some young people are excellent at communicating online but not as much face to face. Do you see this in the young people you know? Is this communication gap important? Why or why not? If you feel it's important, how might you help the young people in your life to boost their face-to-face communication skills?

4. Each of the young people in this book had to reach a point where they decided that it was worth their time and energy to make the world better for others. How can we help to create opportunities for young people to move beyond themselves and to see the needs of others?

5. Do you believe that all young people have the potential to be leaders, or is this a privilege that is reserved for those with specific talents or callings? If you believe that all young people can be leaders, how can adults help them to tap into those talents?

6. All of the young people in this book talked about the importance of motivation when their work became difficult.

How do you distinguish between encouraging and inspiring young people to pursue their dreams and merely pushing them to work for the sake of working hard? Is the difference important?

7. It is tempting to encourage young people to pursue work that you feel is important. For example, some adults might be very passionate about an important cause like helping people who are homeless or providing quality education experiences to middle school girls. But maybe the young people you work with have different interests – like protecting the environment or advancing animal rights. How do you ensure that you are encouraging young people to follow their dreams and not yours? Is this an important distinction? Why?

8. Should young people be required to serve their communities? Why or why not?

9. We hear a lot about the perceived weaknesses of this generation. What are their strengths? How do you think you would fare if you were a young person growing up today? Why?

10. Several of the young people in this book said that the teens they know crave attention from and conversations with adults. What do you think keeps such communication from happening more often? What can adults do to foster dialogue and connections with young people?

11. Which young person in this book could you relate to most? Why?

Reader's Group Discussion Guide
for Youth and Young Adults

1. All of the young people in this book said they thought building connections with like-minded people was important. Who are the people in your life who "speak your language" - sharing your passion for and commitment to improving the world? How could you bring more of these people into your life? How do you maintain those relationships, particularly when you are busy or limited by geography?

2. Doing big things can lead to big criticisms. How do you learn from criticism without letting it discourage you?

3. It is gratifying to get attention for helping others. How should you handle such attention? What are the risks of such attention? What are the benefits?

4. Several of the young people in this book said they saw advantages to doing social justice work as a young person instead of an adult. What are some advantages you see? What are some disadvantages?

5. Some of the young people in this book talked about struggling to set priorities. In some cases, they prioritized their social justice work over their school lives. What do you think of some of the decisions they made? If you had a non-profit organization that was highly successful, would you still see the need to graduate from college? Why or why not?

6. What do you think you still need to know before you can begin your own social justice project? How might you get that information? Who in your life who might be able to point you in the right direction? What other resources might you have to build your skills and get information?

7. Some young people quickly took their projects to the local, regional, national or international levels. What focus would you like an organization to have? Do you think you should start small, or do you think striving to be big from the start is the best path? Why?

8. Are you happy with the relationships you have with the adults in your life? How might you develop stronger relationships if needed? What obstacles might get in the way?

9. What do you think gets in the way when young people are trying to communicate with the adults that are closest to them? What could adults do to make communicating easier? What could young people do to allow for better communication with adults?

10. What do you think keeps young people from working together with other youth more often? What are some obstacles to team building?

11. Do you believe that leaders are born or made? Do you see yourself as a leader? Why or why not?

12. Who are the leaders in your life? Why are they leaders? What skills do they have that you might like to develop? How might you develop them? Who could help you?

13. Which young people did you find most inspirational in this book? Why do you think they appealed to you most?

Reader's Group Discussion Guide for Combined Youth-Adult Book Studies

1. The young people showcased in this book consistently said that the adults in their lives were important to them. What do you think adults need to do to help build positive, meaningful relationships with young people?

2. What obstacles do you think get in the way when young people and the adults in their lives try to communicate? How can you work to overcome them?

3. Some young people said they know youth who pretend they do not want relationships with adults, but really do place value on those connections. Why do you think young people pretend they are not interested in communicating with adults? How might this be changed?

4. What do you think young people want adults to know about their generation?

5. What do adults want young people to know about them?

6. Several young people in this book emphasized the importance of being allowed to make their own mistakes, while still being supported. How do you think this might look? When should supportive adults intervene?

7. What advantages might youth have when doing social justice work? What advantages might adults have?

8. Some of the young people in this book talked about the importance of setting high expectations for youth. How do young people know what expectations adults have set for them? How are these expectations communicated? How might they be communicated differently?

9. What do you see as the benefits of technology among today's youth? What disadvantages might there be to growing up with so much technological access? How can adults help young people to use technology responsibly, or to overcome potential disadvantages of growing up so connected? How can young people assist adults in the use of technology?

10. The young people in this book defined success in a variety of ways. How do you define success? Has your definition changed over time? Why do you think you define success the way you do?

11. Different people have different passions. Some might care most about the environment, while for others, providing food to those in need or helping abused animals may be very important. How might you encourage involvement in your organization, without pressuring people too much to see your passions as more important than their own?

12. Several of the young people in this book talked about the importance of education, both to their current work and in future endeavors. How important do you think a college education is? Do you think it is valuable to get an advanced degree, like a master's or doctorate? Why or why not?

13. How do you think young people choose mentors or role models? What do you think it takes to be a good mentor? What happens when mentors make mistakes or fall short?

14. What challenges do you see in your community that might be addressed through a non-profit organization or through a community service project? What would you need to move forward on this? What role might you take? Who else might have resources, information or contacts to share?

ABOUT THE AUTHORS

The Institute for Educational and Social Justice, co-directed by Dr. Marina V. Gillmore and Dr. Monique R. Henderson, is dedicated to advancing educational and social justice causes by telling stories that build awareness and understanding of educational and social justice issues. Our experience tells us that when dynamic, powerful stories are used to showcase educational and social justice and the work that is being done, people and organizations are inspired to action. Collaboratively, Marina, Monique, and Keith have co-authored one previous book together entitled *Motivation, Education, and Transformation: The Change Agent's Guide to Reaching our Youth and Lifting them Higher.*

Dr. Marina V. Gillmore

Marina has built her professional career around working with youth and teaching, researching, and writing about the transformative power of stories.

A native Californian, Marina has taught English and English Language Development at the high school level and educational and academic research courses at the college level. Marina also has experience as a publications chair, literary journal editor, leadership advisor, head coach, and program and curriculum developer.

Marina holds a doctorate in Leadership for Educational Justice from the University of Redlands. Her dissertation research, situated in the field of social and educational justice, investigated the ways in which teachers' life stories and beliefs inform their teaching practices.

Marina earned a master's in Teacher Education with an English Teaching Credential from Claremont Graduate University, where she conducted award-winning research on the experiences of underserved youth in urban environments. She also earned an honors bachelor's in Literature and History from Claremont McKenna College.

In addition to co-directing the Institute, Marina serves as a university professor and academic consultant, where she works directly with youth in varied capacities. She currently resides with her family in Southern California.

Dr. Monique R. Henderson

Monique has spent more than twenty years analyzing, studying, and advocating for education in Mississippi, Texas, Southern California, and beyond.

An award-winning writer and editor, she has covered public education for numerous newspapers. She also served as Director of Public Relations for the Mississippi Department of Education.

Monique holds a doctorate in Leadership for Educational Justice from the University of Redlands in southern California. She holds a master's in Educational Leadership from the University of Redlands and completed fieldwork in Compton and Perris, California.

She has taught elementary school and also serves as an adjunct professor, teaching future educators, as well as freshman seminar classes. Monique currently resides in the Houston, Texas area, where she works with young people in a variety of roles.

Keith L. Brown

Keith L. Brown, the *Motivator of the Millennium,* has been named one of the top fifty speakers and experts in education today by *Insight Publishing.* Keith is a professional speaker, trainer, author, and educational consultant who has been working for well over a decade empowering youth and adults alike.

Keith's keynotes, workshops, teleconferences, webinars, and books empower nearly 500,000 people annually in schools, supplemental education agencies, colleges and universities, government, corporate settings, faith-based institutions, foundations, and the private sector.

As a student, Keith was once labeled *special ed* and *at risk.* He has overcome these labels and now prides himself on living up to his potential as a *specialty speaker* who *takes risks* and lives the *I'm Possible* message daily. He has authored and co-authored eight previous books and is a proud partner of the *The Institute for Educational and Social Justice.*

ACKNOWLEDGEMENTS

This book would not have been possible without the love and support of our families and friends and the help of some very talented colleagues.

Dr. Marina Gillmore: I would like to first thank my husband, Andy Tomko, for all he does daily to provide the love and support that sustains me. This book has been a long time coming, and from listening to me talk incessantly about this project, to supporting me as I traveled off to conduct interviews, to providing the most serene environment for me to write, reflect, and edit – thank you. I would also like to thank my parents, Keith and Rosanne Gillmore, for being my first and most loyal supporters. My hope is that I continue to reflect back to you all you have taught me about love and compassion and doing right in this world. I would also like to thank my extended family, an incredibly talented and vibrant group, for providing constant reminders of what this life is really all about. And lastly, to Allie, Aiden, Silas, and Thatcher – for the whole of my life, I will work hard to leave this world a little more peaceful, a little more compassionate, and a little kinder for you and the generations that follow.

Dr. Monique Henderson: I would like to thank my husband, Matthew Henderson, for being supportive throughout the writing and editing process, providing food, childcare, and just the right words of encouragement at just the right times. This book truly would not have been possible without you. I would also like to thank the third grade students I have been so privileged to serve at Birnham Woods Elementary in Spring, Texas for the past two school years. You have been a reminder, day after day, that young people really can do amazing, inspiring things. I also would like to thank my own children, Hannah and Hunter Henderson, for their courageous, often selfless examples. Thanks to all of these young people, I see the potential for educational and social justice everywhere. The future really is a bright one.

We, Marina and Monique, would also like to thank the core members of *The Institute for Educational and Social Justice* team who work so selflessly so that we can continue to provide educational outreach, consulting, and writing services to those we serve. Thank you especially to Anne Gremillion, our business manager; Nirmla Flores, our technology director and special projects coordinator; and all of the business partners, consultants, and volunteers who make our work possible.

Keith L. Brown: I would like to humbly thank God for giving me the desire to learn, lift, love, and lead on a daily basis. To my wife, Dr. Wakea (Nikki) Brown – I love and admire your passion for our youth, many of whom you serve daily with the same love and passion you give to our son, nieces, and nephews. You remind the world, and me, daily, "If we can build children, we won't have to repair adults." To my significant, sensational son Keon – you are growing into a young man of purpose and distinction, and the conversations we now have challenge me to expand as both a father and example for your generation. I love you unconditionally, son. To my parents who loved, nurtured, molded, and guided me and kept me involved in extracurricular activities, even when I wanted to be lazy, thank you for making me keep my commitments. To my siblings and other family members who assisted in my growth, thank you for being my "village." To Springfield Gardens United Methodist Church, Springfield Gardens High School, and the Black Spectrum Theatre Company in Queens, New York; Dr. Gerald Deas, my mentor in the Power of One youth leadership organization; Mr. Whitfield Sims, Jr., my director at Black Spectrum; and my beloved Bethel A.M.E. Church and Savannah State University – your pivotal molding of me during my teenage years was a compass for the servant leader I am today. To Dr. R.L. Stevenson, director of the Players by the Sea at Savannah State University, you humbled me and taught me it is just as valuable to "pull the curtains as it is to be on stage as the lead character." To my nieces, nephews, godchildren, teenage cousins, surrogate children in the South Fulton Arrow Youth Council, Omega Mentoring Program, National Lighthouse Foundation, and the thousands I serve nationally and globally, you have opportunities generations before you never had. Live each day with passion. Our future is now in your hands. To all my Partners in Education, both nationally and globally, thank you for dedicating your lives to our youth.

I would also like to thank my *20/20 Enterprises* family – Jolonda T. Greene, booking liaison and licensed psychotherapist; Eboni Stembridge, community relations liaison; Kendall Rucker of the Key One Group and Carl Millender of StarMaxx Media for your audio-visual and technical expertise; and Jasmine Norwood of Visionary Media group for creating professional media to enhance our impact globally. Thank you also to Alicia Obie, key consultant; J.R. Henderson, founder and executive director of the National

Lighthouse Foundation; Leon Carter, whose affirmations have helped many students love themselves, believe in themselves, and be proud of themselves as geniuses; Tykeisha Lewis, founder of Educationally Speaking; Caryn Brown Piankhi of Inspired Creations; and Virlinda Holmes and Vanna Walker Byrd, our on-site motivators and sales team. Further thanks go to our past and present student interns – thank you for reaching beyond your grasp. And to D. Jean Brannan, past COO of the Sickle Cell Foundation of Georgia, thank you for having faith in me way back when I was beginning my professional speaking journey. To all these wonderful individuals whom I am indebted to and inspired by, I proclaim, "G-double-O-D J-O-B... Good job! Good job!"

Collectively, the authors would also like to thank the following individuals and organizations who helped turn our vision for this project into a reality. Thank you to Ahmad Meradji and his team at Booklogix for your professional publishing services. Thank you to Carol Hanley and Carrie Tomko for your invaluable editing support. Thank you to Frederick Courtright of the Permissions Company for your keen attention to detail. Thank you to Dr. Robert Denham for believing wholeheartedly in this project and for writing a foreword that inspires us to keep the mission of social and educational justice central to our work. Thank you to the families, mentors, and other change agents who have affected so dramatically the lives of the young people we've featured in these pages. The words are theirs, but their messages, and confidence, and belief in the beauty of this world are due, in large part, to the "villages" that raised them – and continue to raise them, lift them up, and let them soar. Thank you.

And lastly, we've said it before, but we have to say it again. Thank you a thousand times over to the "significant six" – Joe, MaryPat, Max, Shaylee, Jordan, and R.L. for sharing with us your stories and enthusiasm for this project. We have been enriched by the opportunity to work with you and you have inspired us to continue this life-long journey of service and leadership. You have set in motion an example that will be followed by millions globally. We are so honored to work with, inspire, and be inspired by you. This book, this labor of love, is for you. May your stories continue – for years to come – to remind us all of the incredible power of youth.

ADDITIONAL RESOURCES

If you would like to learn more about the work of the remarkable young people featured in this book, we encourage you to visit their websites and reach out to them via social media outlets. Their websites are as follows:

> Joe Gigunito: www.whereisthelove.org
> Jordan Howard: www.jordaninspires.com
> MaryPat Hector: www.marypathector.webs.com
> Max Wallack: www.puzzlestoremember.org
> R.L. Wilson: www.facebook.com/bait.langston
> Shaylee Hatch: www.thetemporaryhomefoundation.org

Also, if this book has spoken to you in some way, please share it with others. Please also stop by our websites at www.keithlbrown.com and www.instituteforedandsocialjustice.com and reach out to us on Facebook (search: Keith L Brown1911 and The Institute for Educational and Social Justice).

The authors of this book are available for consulting, keynote speaking, staff development, school-wide assemblies, book discussions, parent seminars, and other special events. Please visit our websites or contact us by email for more information.

A percentage of proceeds from this book will go directly to support the efforts of the young people featured within these pages. Thank you for purchasing this book so that we can continue to pay it forward.